EERO SAARINEN

W.W. NORTON & COMPANY NEW YORK AND LONDON IN ASSOCIATION WITH THE LIBRARY OF CONGRESS

BUILDINGS FROM THE **BALTHAZAR KORAB** ARCHIVE

EERO SAARINEN

EDITED BY DAVID G. DE LONG AND C. FORD PEATROSS

NORTON / LIBRARY OF CONGRESS VISUAL SOURCEBOOKS IN ARCHITECTURE, DESIGN & ENGINEERING

Note: The digital ID numbers given to the Korab images and
Saarinen building plans have the prefix LC-DIG. Use these
numbers to access the images at www.loc.gov.

PAGE 1 00.001. Saint Louis Gateway Arch. (krb-00175)
PAGE 2 00.002. General Motors Technical Center. (krb-00077)
PAGE 6 00.003. Miller House terrace. (krb-00313)

Manufacturing by Colorprint Offset
Book design by Abigail Sturges
Production manager: Leeann Graham

Library of Congress Cataloging-in-Publication Data
Eero Saarinen : buildings from the Balthazar Korab archive /
edited by David G. De Long and C. Ford Peatross.
    p. cm. — (Norton/Library of Congress visual sourcebooks
in architecture, design and engineering)
    Includes bibliographical references and index.
    ISBN 978-0-393-73223-8 (hardcover)
    1. Saarinen, Eero, 1910-1961—Themes, motives. 2. Modern
movement (Architecture) 3. Korab, Balthazar—Photograph
collections. I. De Long, David Gilson, 1939- II. Peatross,
C. Ford. III. Saarinen, Eero, 1910-1961.
    NA737.S28A4 2008
    720.92—dc22
                                            2007000446
ISBN 13: 978-0-393-73223-8

W. W. Norton & Company, Inc., 500 Fifth Avenue,
New York, N.Y. 10110, www.wwnorton.com

W. W. Norton & Company Ltd., Castle House,
75/76 Wells Street, London W1T 3QT

0 9 8 7 6 5 4 3 2 1

Center for Architecture, Design and Engineering
The Norton/Library of Congress Visual Sourcebooks in Architecture, Design and Engineering series is a project of the Center for
Architecture, Design and Engineering in the Library of Congress,
established through a bequest from the distinguished American
architect Paul Rudolph. The Center's mission is not only to support the preservation of the Library's enormously rich collections
in these subject areas, but also to increase public knowledge of
and access to them. Paul Rudolph hoped that others would join
him in supporting these efforts. To further this progress, and to
support additional projects such as this one, the Library of
Congress is therefore pleased to accept contributions to the Center
for Architecture, Design and Engineering Fund or memorials in
Mr. Rudolph's name as additions to the Paul Rudolph Trust.
    For further information on the Center for American
Architecture, Design and Engineering, you may visit its Web
site: www.loc.gov/rr/print/adecenter/adecent.html

C. FORD PEATROSS
*Curator of Architecture,
Design and Engineering*

The Center for Architecture, Design and Engineering and the Publishing Office of the Library of Congress are pleased to join with W. W. Norton & Company to publish the pioneering series of the Norton / Library of Congress Visual Sourcebooks in Architecture, Design and Engineering.

Based on the unparalleled collections of the Library of Congress, this series of handsomely illustrated books draws from the collections of the nation's oldest federal cultural institution and the largest library in the world, with more than 134 million items on approximately 615 miles of bookshelves. The collections include more than 20.5 million books, 2.8 million recordings, 12 million photographs, 5.2 million maps, and 59 million manuscripts.

The subjects of architecture, design, and engineering are threaded throughout the rich fabric of this vast archive, and the books in this new series will serve not only to introduce researchers to the illustrations selected by their authors, but also to build pathways to adjacent and related materials, and even entire archives—to millions of photographs, drawings, prints, views, maps, rare publications, and written information in the general and special collections of the Library of Congress, much of it unavailable elsewhere.

Each volume serves as a portal to the collections, providing a treasury of select visual material (much of it in the public domain) for students, scholars, teachers, researchers, historians of art, architecture, design, and technology, and practicing architects, engineers, and designers of all kinds.

The DVD accompanying this volume includes reference-quality, downloadable versions of most of the illustrations. It offers a direct link to the Library's online, searchable catalogs and image files, including the hundreds of thousands of high-resolution photographs, measured drawings, and data files in the Historic American Buildings Survey, Historic American Engineering Record, and the Historic American Landscape Survey. The Library's Web site has rapidly become one of the most popular and valuable locations on the Internet, visited 111 million times in 2006 and comprising more than 184 terrabytes of knowledge, and serving audiences ranging from school children to the most advanced scholars throughout the world, with a potential usefulness that has only begun to be explored.

Among the subjects to be covered in this series are building types, materials, and details; historical periods and movements; landscape architecture and garden design; interior and ornamental design and furnishings; and industrial design. This volume is the first in the series that is monographic, in that it focuses on the work of a single architect, Eero Saarinen, and a single architectural photographer, Balthazar Korab, both of whom did much to shape our vision of American architecture during the second half of the twentieth century. We thank Balthazar Korab for his generosity in donating his original photographic negatives and transparencies, and architect Kevin Roche for his gift of archival material from the Office of Eero Saarinen & Associates, without which this handsome publication would not have been possible. *Eero Saarinen: Buildings From The Balthazar Korab Archive* is another exemplar of the goals and possibilities on which this series is based.

JAMES H. BILLINGTON
The Librarian of Congress

CONTENTS

REDISCOVERING EERO SAARINEN

DEPARTURES FROM ORTHODOX MODERNISM

Eero Saarinen (00.004) came to prominence in the 1950s, challenging architectural conventions of his time with new forms that attracted international attention. In the United States, he seemed poised to fulfill the postwar expectation of a new architecture and become the country's leading architect, perhaps even surpassing both Frank Lloyd Wright (1867–1959) and Ludwig Mies van der Rohe (1886–1969). Yet his untimely death in 1961, at age fifty-one, cut short that promise, and changing fashions in the years that followed distracted students and critics alike from the study of his work. Now, like the contents of a newly opened time capsule, his buildings can be examined anew to reveal fresh insights.[1]

Even in the 1950s, some remained unconvinced by Saarinen's architecture, questioning what they regarded as willful stylistic diversity in his work.[2] Allan Temko, in a brief monograph published just after Saarinen's death, used such terms as "arbitrary" and "subjective" to describe some of the buildings.[3] Nearly twenty years later, Peter Papademetriou continued to find such diversity troubling, writing that Saarinen's work "never evolved into a single aesthetic, nor did it evidence the 'signature' consistency of other artists and architects."[4]

Far from being troubled, I would argue that such diversity constitutes the very strength of Saarinen's work. Those baffled by its seeming inconsistencies are perhaps too closely bound by the current notion of style as a matter of choice, as something used to "style" a building almost in the manner of applied decoration.[5] Seemingly lost to view is Meyer Schapiro's magisterial definition of style as a reflection of period, as a unifying reflection of cultural aspiration.[6] In this sense Saarinen's work is very consistent indeed, for it reflects the quest of modernist architects to seek new forms for new functions, and to incorporate new materials and new technologies into their work as an effective means of such expression. In this larger sense, Saarinen's work reflects a period of inquiry that underlies modern architecture, something that Sarah Williams Goldhagen has described as a vital discourse of the time.[7] Thus, in its very diversity Saarinen's work honors underlying principles, principles that help define modernism and its limits.

Like many of his generation, Saarinen was frustrated by the limits of orthodox modernism. Rigidly defined by Henry-Russell Hitchcock and Philip Johnson in 1932 as the International Style, it dictated strict adherence to simple geometries, untextured surfaces, and a light, seemingly weightless volumetric expression. As seen in the work of Mies van der Rohe, its leading American adherent, space was to be open and continuous, and any suggestion of applied ornament was totally rejected.[8] An alternative, more varied, and more personal modernism advocated by Frank Lloyd Wright and his followers struck many at the time as equally restrictive and seemed also to have run its course.

Regarding his impatience with orthodox modernism, Saarinen wrote:

> I feel strongly that modern architecture is in danger of falling into a mold too quickly—too rigid a mold. What once was a great hope for a great new period of architecture has somehow become an automatic application of the same formula over and over again everywhere. . . . I align myself humbly with Le Corbusier and against Mies van der Rohe.[9]

He questioned open interiors, saying, "Today many of us have come back to much more 'closed' plans, where rooms are really rooms with four walls."[10] He suggested that mass and texture could again be justified, saying in reference to his design for the CBS Building in New York (1960–1965), "it should look permanent. I think too

much modern architecture is flimsy-looking. . . . Neutral buildings do not stimulate man's imagination."[11]

Louis I. Kahn (1901–74), who would surpass Saarinen in terms of reputation during the second half of the twentieth century, used similar words to question orthodox modernism.[12] This impelled him to reconnect with underlying principles of ancient architecture as a fundamental means of redirecting architecture, and he produced buildings that made modernism seem outdated. Others, with less struggle, enriched their modernist vocabularies with decorative motifs. Robert Venturi famously pilloried this more surface-bound approach:

> A false complexity has recently countered the false simplicity of an earlier Modern architecture. It promotes an architecture of symmetrical picturesqueness—which Minoru Yamasaki calls "serene"—but it represents a new formalism as unconnected with experience as the former cult of simplicity.[13]

In seeking to free himself from the constraints of orthodox modernism, Saarinen moved in a different direction. For him, inspiration seemed to lie with early variants of modern architecture, especially those with expressionist themes that came to be echoed in his mature work. By then, those early sources of a more diverse modernism had been largely forgotten in the rush to embrace the stricter tenets of the International Style. In renewing these themes, Saarinen challenged the conventions of orthodox modernism, yet not the broader conventions of modernism itself. Instead he sought to stretch even those broader conventions so as to achieve his ends.

In the 1950s, Saarinen also spoke of the need to enrich architecture with meaningful expression:

> what is the purpose of architecture? . . . much more than its utilitarian meaning—to provide shelter for man's activities on earth. It is certainly that, but I believe it has a much more fundamental role to play for man, almost a religious one. . . . to fulfill his belief in the nobility of existence. . . . How can the whole building convey emotionally the purpose and meaning of the building? Conveying significant meaning is part of the inspirational purpose of architecture. . . . We need an expanded vocabulary because modern architecture is now mature enough to think about bigger problems of expression.[14]

In leaving deeper issues of modernism unquestioned, Saarinen fell short of Kahn's more fundamental redefinition of architecture. Yet major examples of the late-twentieth and early-twenty-first century architecture, such as buildings by Frank Gehry and Zaha Hadid, have more recently reconnected with expressionist themes of the early twentieth century, positioning Saarinen as a critical link.

00.005. Community House, Fenton, Michigan, 1937–38. (krb-00002)

A QUEST FOR MEANINGFUL DESIGN

Eero Saarinen spent his childhood years in Finland, where he was born in 1910 and where he grew up at Hvitträsk, the great country estate of his parents that reflected their grounding in the Arts and Crafts movement. His father, Eliel Saarinen (1873–1950), was regarded at the time as Finland's greatest architect, and his mother, Louise 'Loja' Gesellius Saarinen (1879–1968), was an important weaver and an artist in her own right. In 1923, when Eero Saarinen was thirteen years old, the family relocated to the United States, and in 1925 they settled in Bloomfield Hills, Michigan, where in the years that followed Eliel Saarinen designed the famous Cranbrook campus of related institutions that came to include the Cranbrook School for Boys (1926–30), the Cranbrook Academy of Art, which he led for many years (1926–42), the Kingswood School for Girls (1929–31), and the Cranbrook Institute of Science (initiated in 1931, but only completed in 1937).

In accord with Arts and Crafts principles advocated at Cranbrook, both Eero and his older sister, Pipsan (Eva-Lisa Saarinen, 1905–79), were involved in design projects at an early age. For Eero, this led to furniture designs for

00.006. First Christian Church (originally Tabernacle Church of Christ), Columbus, Indiana, 1939–42, exterior. (krb-00003)

00.007. First Christian Church, interior. (krb-00004)

the Kingswood School for Girls (1929–31), part of the Cranbrook complex. While engaged in this project, Saarinen studied sculpture in Paris (1929–30), as had his mother before him (1902–03). But, soon after his return to the United States, he entered Yale University to study architecture; surviving examples of his student work seem unremarkable.[15] Following graduation from Yale in 1934 he traveled to Egypt, the Middle East, and Europe, ending in Helsinki, where he worked in the office of Karl Ecklund. While there he prepared numerous facade studies of the Swedish Theater, a commission that his father had once held with Ecklund, but that Ecklund then held alone. The almost indiscernible variations among these studies suggest a mind obsessed with minor detail.[16]

In 1936, Saarinen returned to Bloomfield Hills and entered into partnership with his father. At first he seems to have had little effect on Eliel Saarinen's conservative modernism, as reflected in their joint design for the Community House in Fenton, Michigan (1937–38; 00.005). But in later projects a clearer, more radical modernism soon began to surface, seen to advantage in the widely acclaimed First Christian Church (originally Tabernacle Church of Christ, Columbus, Indiana, 1939–42; 00.006 and 00.007). It recalls contemporary

Finnish work by Alvar Aalto (1898–1976) and, more closely, churches by Erik Bryggmann (1891–1955). Letters written by Eero Saarinen while in Finland include sketches of similar churches by Bryggmann, documenting his admiration for these sources. These letters were addressed to Florence Schust (Florence Schust Knoll Bassett, b. 1917)[17], an early graduate of the Kingswood School for Girls who later studied at the Cranbrook Academy of Art and is now better known by her first married name, Florence Knoll. She achieved fame as the chief designer at Knoll Associates, Inc., one of the world's foremost manufacturers of modern furniture; Eero Saarinen would be among several leading architects who designed for the firm.

There seems little doubt that Saarinen's enthusiasm for modernist architecture surpassed that of his father, and it seems probable that the more modernist designs emanating from the firm in these years were more the work of Eero than Eliel. This is supported by evidence from Ralph Rapson, who, as an architecture student working in the Saarinen office from 1938 to 1940, witnessed the quite different authorships of two designs of the period: the Cranbrook Museum and Library (1938–42) and the Smithsonian Gallery of Art (Washington, D.C.,

1939–41; unbuilt).[18] Rapson recalled that Eero had little to do with the Cranbrook Museum (a massive, richly textured building), and that Eliel disdained Eero's design for the sleekly modern Smithsonian Gallery, shaking his head "no" as he stood behind Eero at his desk.[19]

With the final design of the General Motors Technical Center, Eero's phase of orthodox modernism, partly revealed by such earlier designs as the Wermuth house (Fort Wayne, Indiana, 1941–42), reached maturity. The firm had received the commission in 1945, and a design of that year with futuristic, streamlined buildings is often credited to Eliel, but its resemblance to Norman Bel Geddes's (1893–1953) General Motors Pavilion at the 1939 New York World's Fair, on which Eero had briefly worked in the summer of 1938, suggests otherwise.[20] Evidence indicates that work on a second proposal was under way by 1946, but the final scheme is more often dated to 1948; construction, delayed by wartime shortages, began in 1949 and was completed in 1956.[21]

As widely noted, the campus of some twenty-five crisply detailed low, freestanding buildings (see 01.001–01.068) most obviously recalls Mies van der Rohe's Illinois Institute of Technology campus in Chicago (1939–). Yet important differences distinguish Saarinen's design. The central lake (nearly 600 by 1,800 feet), animated by extensive fountains, provides a degree of focus absent in Mies's design, and such dramatic features as the water tower and domed pavilion add a degree of architectural richness absent in that famous prototype. Planes of brightly colored brick—explained as a means of identifying functional clusters—also differentiate Saarinen's essay in orthodox modernism from its famous prototype.

Saarinen described the Center as having five major clusters: research, process development, engineering, styling, and a service center in addition to a central restaurant. He described his design as "based on steel—the metal of the automobile. . . . we tried to give the architecture the precise, well-made look which is a proud characteristic of industrial America."[22] He seemed particularly proud of new building technologies that he incorporated into its design:

> General Motors represents the first significant installation of laminated panels and the first use anywhere of a uniquely thin porcelain-faced sandwich panel which is a complete prefabricated wall for both exterior and interior. . . . The ceilings in the drafting rooms are the first developed completely luminous ceilings. . . . Perhaps the greatest gift to the building industry is the development of the neoprene gasket weather seal, which holds fixed glass and porcelain enamel panels to their aluminum frames. It is truly windproof and waterproof.[23]

Such technological innovations, much noticed at the time, have continued to figure in discussions of the design.[24]

Dramatic interior features further enrich the modernist vocabulary, none more so than the circular stair in the Research and Development Administration Building, often photographed in relation to the custom furniture that Saarinen designed in collaboration with Florence Knoll (see 01.061–01.065). Saarinen rationalized the stair as deriving from the technologically efficient structure of a bicycle wheel. Its finely crafted details—typical of details throughout the complex—reflect the Arts and Crafts grounding of his Cranbrook background. Yet it goes beyond handcrafting. Parallel with designs by other Cranbrook students—most notably furniture by Charles and Ray Eames (1907–78; 1912–88) and by Harry Bertoia (1915–78)—it seems to have achieved the elusive "art and craft of the machine" that Frank Lloyd Wright had so fervently sought in his own work.[25] And Bertoia's sculptural screen adds special presence to the restaurant, a record of Saarinen's ongoing collaboration with artists (see 01.066–01.068).

Published accounts have consistently credited Eero Saarinen with primary design responsibility of the GM Technical Center, a reflection of his aging father's gradual transfer of responsibility and of the two men's increasing tendency to assume individual control over selected projects. Eliel Saarinen continued to direct smaller commissions, as seen in the Stephens College Chapel (1946–50, unbuilt) and the Christ Church Lutheran (Minneapolis, Minnesota, 1947–49). Both show the elder Saarinen continuing to explore currents of a conservative, somewhat massive modernism.

Affirming their different approaches, Eliel and Eero Saarinen submitted independent entries into the competition for the Jefferson National Expansion Memorial, held in 1947. Eliel Saarinen's monumental arch recalls his solution for the open entrance pavilion joining the Cranbrook Museum and Library, but at a much larger scale (00.008). Eero Saarinen's lithe, celebratory arch—which won the competition—spoke of a newer age. Now known as the Saint Louis Gateway Arch, it was at last essentially completed in 1965 after an arduous sequence of changes and delays. By then its design had long been celebrated (see 02.001–02.017). Rising to a height of 630 feet, the reinforced concrete core is clad with reflective stainless steel that seems to further reduce the weight of an already visually weightless form. It has become the "triumphal arch for our age" that Saarinen intended.[26] The arch takes the shape of a catenary curve (a structurally efficient profile generated by a hanging chain or heavy cord that is then inverted; Saarinen's is weighted rather than pure) and frames vistas to the historic core of Saint Louis and to the West itself. Beneath the arch, a monumental stair echoes the curve of the arch above (see 02.022). With his characteristic attention to detail, Saarinen had a full-scale model built adjacent to his office so as to test its unusual profile; a famous picture shows him trying it for himself (see 02.005). Louis I. Kahn, who greatly admired Saarinen's solution, later lamented that his own entry was so mired in the complicated details of the competition program that it justly deserved its failed status, while Saarinen, by contrast, had the genius to rise above the program and concentrate instead on an iconic image.[27]

In 1950, Irwin Miller, then head of the prominent family that had earlier commissioned the firm's First Christian Church, reestablished the family's patronage with two additional commissions. They proved to be the first of many commissions to leading architects awarded through family support, with results that have made Columbus, Indiana, an architectural mecca.[28]

For the Miller family's summer retreat in Canada, Saarinen designed a luxurious house in Ontario (1950–52; see 03.001–03.018). Located north of Toronto and encompassing three lakes within its bounds, this area attracted people of wealth from the beginning of the twentieth century and continues, in the twenty-first, to be a place of luxurious escape.[29] Responding to a terrain that has been likened to that of the Adirondacks, Saarinen designed an informal, camp-like lodge with angled wings built of richly textured stone and wood, a modern interpretation of rusticity. Broad terraces link the house to its setting, while sleekly contemporary furniture both

within and without—much of it designed by fellow Cranbrook students Charles and Ray Eames—affirm its mid-twentieth-century date.

Within Columbus itself and in striking contrast to the surrounding buildings of its main street, Saarinen designed a glass pavilion for the Irwin Union Bank & Trust Company (1950–54; see 04.001–04.014). It sustains themes being explored in the General Motors Technical Center, with a dramatically framed stair and with domed shapes, the latter not seen in isolation as a single building but as a series of regularly spaced low domes that recall an Ottoman mosque. From above, they enliven the broad expanse of the flat roof; inside, they configure the open interior with graceful, volume-enhancing presence.

In two quite different commissions of 1950 for the Massachusetts Institute of Technology—the Kresge Auditorium and Chapel (1950–55, see 05.001–05.020)—Saarinen embarked upon a series of more striking departures from orthodox modernism. Completed just before the General Motors Technical Center, they drew widespread attention and did much to establish Saarinen as a major innovator of his time. Yet Saarinen explained each of these departures according to modernist logic, a reminder that he left the basic rules of his time unquestioned.

For the Kresge Auditorium, Saarinen utilized thin shell concrete construction, a new technology of the time that could produce varied, yet structurally efficient, forms. In

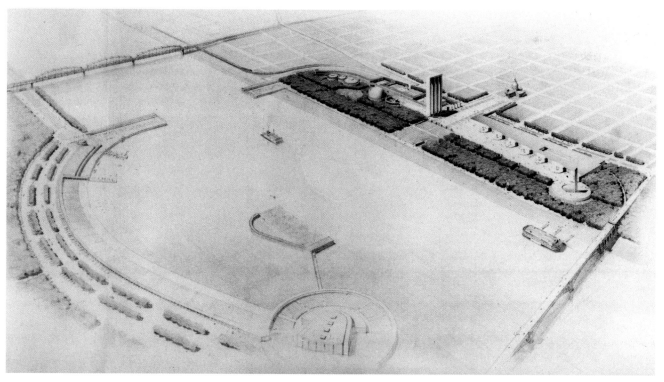

00.008. Jefferson National Expansion Memorial competition entry, St. Louis, Missouri, 1947, unbuilt; Eliel Saarinen. From *Design in America: The Cranbrook Vision, 1925–1950* (New York: Harry N. Abrams, 1983), perspective. (N330.B55 C74)

shaping another design, Saarinen had reportedly upended his breakfast grapefruit, thus beginning with a dome, then sliced away sections to model his concept.[30] The same could be said of the Kresge Auditorium, where this kind of slicing effected several things: in plan, it produced the triangular shape that Saarinen believed to be ideal for an auditorium; in elevation, it created broad segmental arches that allowed natural openings for both windows and doors; and structurally, it exploited the efficiency of thin shell construction while eliminating the need for continuous support at the base. A podium of low steps emphasized the bold simplicity of the unusual form. Yet Saarinen's logic was sorely tested; neither the triangular shape nor the domed roof were acoustically effective, leading to later modifications by engineers at MIT.[31]

Saarinen's design for the Kresge Chapel yielded a more workable result. Perhaps partly inspired by his father's circular design for the Stephens College Chapel, he, too, began with a circular enclosure. He explained:

> since this is, uniquely, a non-denominational chapel, it was essential to create an atmosphere which was not derived from a particular religion, but from basic spiritual feelings. A dark interior seemed right—an interior completely separated from the outside world. . . . The interior was curved, both for acoustical reasons and to give the space a lack of sharp definition and an increased sense of turning inward.[32]

In response to the building's context, Saarinen chose bricks that loosely resembled those of nearby MIT buildings, exaggerating their texture with randomly projected blocks. At the base, low arches of varied size lift the cylindrical form above an encircling moat, adding elements expressive of a wall-bearing structure.

To judge by accounts published at the time, the interior proved to be the most captivating aspect of the design. It seemed to achieve the very atmosphere of timelessness that Saarinen sought, one detached from a standard modernist vocabulary and sensuously evocative without recourse to specific historic quotation. A single skylight animates the altar screen by Harry Bertoia, and glazed segments of the floor at the perimeter, behind a low, undulating wall, produce a subdued, flickering glow (see 05.019–05.020). Outside, the sculptural spire by Theodore Rosak (see 05.013–05.015) was less successfully integrated, yet, like the altar screen, it affirmed Saarinen's continuing commitment to collaboration as encouraged by his father at Cranbrook.

Other designs originating in the early 1950s were more conservative and drew less attention, yet are not without interest. For the Milwaukee Art Museum (designed as the Milwaukee War Memorial, Milwaukee, Wisconsin, 1952–57; 06.001–06.015), Saarinen developed box-like shapes of concrete that enclosed specific functions while providing structural support. He arranged these stark, cantilevered boxes on raised supports that clearly defined separate levels. As he described it:

> the building consists of three parts. One is the base, which builds the mass up to the city level and contains an art museum; the second, on city level, is the memorial court with a pool. . . . The third part is the superstructure, cantilevered outward thirty feet in three directions, which contains the meeting halls and offices of the veterans' organizations.[33]

The more subdued structure of the University of Michigan School of Music (Ann Arbor, Michigan, 1952–56; see 07.001–07.011) enclosed an even more articulated building, with individual elements defined in an almost diagrammatic manner. Saarinen designed it while working on a master plan for the university, one of his several large-scale planning commissions. Typically not only for Saarinen but for most designers as well, such planning efforts yielded little in terms of realized construction, for changing priorities tended to compromise any initial vision.

During these productive years, there were few commissions for individual dwellings. In 1945, Saarinen had collaborated with Charles and Ray Eames on designs for Case Study Houses Nos. 8 and 9—two in the famous series of prototypical designs sponsored by John Entenza, all presented in *Arts and Architecture*, the path-breaking journal Entenza edited (and published) from 1938 to 1967. Yet drawings in the Eameses' office suggest that Saarinen's involvement was slight.[34] Then, in 1953, Irwin Miller gave Saarinen the commission for his family's primary dwelling in Columbus. Completed in 1957 (see 08.001–08.040), it stands as one of Saarinen's major achievements, an elegant composition that infuses mid-century modernism with uncharacteristic richness. Designed as a largely open pavilion with private suites at each corner, it incorporates elegantly refined materials and luxuriously crafted details. Sculpturally spare steel column shafts terminate in open capitals with cross-shaped profiles that link to regularly spaced linear skylights, creating an effect in which light itself seems to delineate component parts of the house, suggesting separation without physical barriers. Alexander Girard (1907–93), the renowned American designer, collaborated on the interiors, and photographs taken over time show how seasonal moods were effected in a time-honored manner with changeable coverings and accessories: bright reds and oranges for winter, whites for summer. The recessed seating area recalls a similar device that Saarinen and Eams had earlier used in Case Study House No. 9 (00.009). On the walls behind, changing art works record the family's active collecting. Dan Kiley (Daniel Urban Kiley, 1912–2004) designed the expansive gardens that give the house special prominence, and there, too, are works of art, each well positioned within landscaped

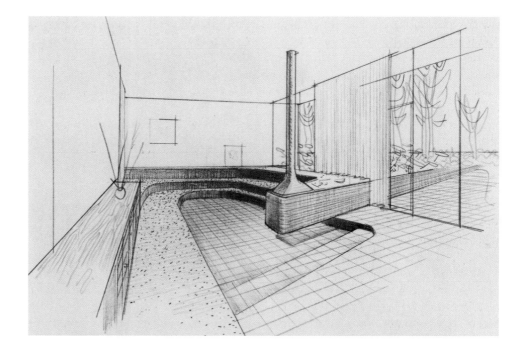

features so as to further enhance the setting. Rarely has the American Midwest been so persuasively shaped.

Another Midwest commission led to different results. For the Concordia Theological Seminary (designed as the Concordia Senior College, Fort Wayne, Indiana, 1953–58; see 09.001–09.014), Saarinen developed a small, informal campus of spare buildings that differ markedly from the Miller house in Columbus, yet in their own way they are also evocative of place. Saarinen focused on the contemplative nature of the seminary in his descriptions:

> we wanted to create an environment appropriate to the intellectual and spiritual training of young men who would go on to professional studies in theology. . . . the village concept: a group of buildings which would have a quiet, unified environment into which the students could withdraw to find a complete, balanced life and yet one which was related to the outside world.[35]

The tall A-frame chapel dominates the composition, its triangular shape echoed by the brick patterns of its end walls. Similar patterns amplify the lower pitches of surrounding buildings, relieving the otherwise plain shapes that stand independently on broad, landscaped plazas.

Problems of context that seemed to call for details sympathetic to traditional surroundings may have frustrated Saarinen in these years. In an effort to relate to Gothic revival buildings on the University of Chicago's campus, he devised a decorative facade of angled glass planes for its new Law School, a superficial gesture in an otherwise well-massed building (1955–60, see 10.001–10.006). The United States chancellery in London (1955–60, see 11.001–11.021) must have proved even more trouble-some, at least to judge by the countless facade studies that Saarinen prepared, yet the results were finer. Wanting to relate in terms of scale and detail to the low neo-Georgian buildings then being erected around the Grosvenor Square setting they shared, yet apparently determined to do so in a structurally rational manner rather than through applied details, Saarinen developed a facade of interlocking, carefully proportioned windows in which the frames themselves were structural. As he said:

> We sought harmony in various ways. The mass and general cornice height—the silhouette against the sky—conform to those of the buildings in the future square. There is continuity of material: the Portland stone which is trim and ornament on the red brick pseudo-Georgian buildings becomes *the* material for the embassy.

Continuing, he described the building's context and his reaction to it:

> . . . a general scale set up by the size of windows and decorations on the pseudo-Georgian facades. The same scale, only slightly bolder, has been sought in the embassy facade by the structural system that forms it. This wall structure of coupled precise concrete columns placed alternately above each other creates a fenestration that is related to that of the other buildings. This structural system also gave the desired plastic quality.[36]

With commissions less encumbered by setting, and for uses less demanding of official image, Saarinen must have been more at ease, as can be illustrated with the IBM Manufacturing and training facility (Rochester, Minnesota, 1956–58; see 12.001–12.029). There, on a remote site and with a flexibility reflective of his essentially modernist approach, he could return to a purer expression of form appropriate to the building's industrial purpose. Yet with his characteristic questioning of a standard, uniform solution—also reflective of his modernist approach—he managed to inject special life into the long, low facades by combining glass of two colors to achieve an effect of bold stripes. Reflecting the stern, narrow standards of the time, Temko complained:

> the arbitrary division of the spandrels into areas of dark and light blue (signifying no internal dispositions) is patently unjustified. As at General Motors, Saarinen again relied on decorative color to achieve vitality that would have been better attained by structural means.[37]

The commission was one of several for industrial and corporate campuses that came to Saarinen as a result of his success with the General Motors Technical Center.[38]

For a second IBM commission—the Thomas J. Watson Research Center (Yorktown Heights, New York, 1956–61; 13.001–13.012)—Saarinen began with a scheme of rectangular pavilions neatly arranged in a modified checkerboard fashion, like those of the Rochester complex. Yet as he developed the design he gave consideration to the hillside site—quite different in nature than the flatter Rochester setting—and to the less industrial function of the Yorktown project. The individual pavilions of the earlier design gave way to one long, gently curved structure that reinforced its hillside site. As he explained its layout,

> all laboratories and offices are put in interior space and the window-periphery is left for the main corridors. . . . The building was curved in a crescent, following the configuration of the hill. It is planned so that this curve can embrace the hill even further by extending the crescent in its future expansion. . . . This curving shape, with the marquee at the center, is emphasized by long, raking fieldstone walls. The end of each of these is accented with a sculpture commissioned from Seymour Lipton.[39]

In a third commission of 1956 for a corporate client—the Deere and Company Headquarters (Moline, Illinois, 1956–64; 16.001–16.032)—Saarinen dealt more decisively with the site and with the building's primary material, a newly available steel marketed as Cor-Ten. Set within a lushly landscaped setting where it bridged between two hills, the building became one with its site, gently defining one edge of an expansive lake that reflected its intricately detailed façade. The steel that Saarinen selected for both its structure and open screen of sun shades seemed calculated to celebrate the material of the company's farm machinery, as Saarinen himself suggested. It also provided economies of construction, for the steel, engineered so it developed a self-protecting layer of corrosion, required no added layer of fire protection, and could thus be left exposed. This Saarinen exploited to its fullest, detailing each component with exacting care, even erecting a full-scale bay to study its intricate proportions. It set a high standard for the many suburban office complexes that seemed to become almost a corporate cliché in the years that followed, yet its elegant image again provoked critical dismay:

> one must . . . ponder the subjective inner convictions which caused the architect, in his last important design in metal and glass, to resort to overstatement—exaggeration—in the headquarters for Deere & Company . . . 'an iron building for a farm machinery manufacturer,' was Saarinen's summary of the concept. The phrase is straightforward enough, but it implies a welling romanticism . . .[40]

Two other commissions of 1956—the Ingalls Hockey Rink and the TWA Terminal—provided opportunities for Saarinen to address building types new to his practice and relatively new to architecture as well. In each, the challenge of the special function to be housed led to expressive results, results justified as an exploration of a new building technology uniquely suited to the problem at hand.

For the David S. Ingalls Hockey Rink at Yale University (New Haven, Connecticut, 1956–58; 14.001–14.007), Saarinen developed a structure of suspended steel cables that joined sympathetically to the central arch along the building's spine. The building could even be described as a sculptural portrait of the game itself. Saarinen described his concept in more rational terms:

> The great spine-like concrete arch is the dominant theme. We wanted it to be both structurally effective and beautiful. We decided to counteract the normally downward aspect of the arch form by making the ends sweep up in cantilevered extensions. The soaring form was further emphasized by the lighting fixture at the entrance end, which we commissioned from a sculptor, Oliver Andrews, so it would have expressive as well as functional meaning. . . . The cables, which were suspended in catenary curves from the central arch, stretch down to their anchorage in the exterior walls on each side. These curved walls are counterparts to the arch: they are in plan as the shape of the center arch is in section.[41]

Not long before embarking on the design of the Ingalls Hockey Rink, Saarinen had spoken of an obligation to rationalize such form: "we should proceed into the field of plastic form with caution. Plastic form uncontrolled by structure rings a hollow note."[42] Yet, typical of criticism in the years following Saarinen's death, Yale's famous architectural historian, Vincent Scully, remained unconvinced: " . . . it embodied a good deal that was wrong with American architecture in the mid-1950's:

exhibitionism, structural pretension, self-defeating urbanistic arrogance."[43] Saarinen's break with architectural conventions of his time was far from easy.

For the Trans World Airlines Terminal at John F. Kennedy International Airport (originally Idlewild; New York City, 1956–62; 15.001–15.032), Saarinen went further in his exploration of plastic form, achieving one of his most notable works. Edgar Kaufmann, jr., one of the most discerning critics of the time, described it as "one of the crisp peaks . . . of modern architecture. . . . [and] the best testimony why, when Saarinen died, architecture lost one of its chief American masters.[44]

Saarinen began somewhat cautiously with a more conventional form (see 15.042–15.043), but soon embarked upon studies in which the building was literally sculpted in model form (see 15.009). He made his motivations clear:

> [we sought] a building in which the architecture itself would express the drama and specialness and excitement of travel. Thus, we wanted the architecture to reveal the terminal, not as a static, enclosed place, but as a place of movement and transition. . . . [the structure] consists essentially of four interacting barrel vaults of slightly different shapes, supported on four Y-shaped columns. Together, these vaults make a vast concrete shell, fifty feet high and 315 feet long. . . . The shapes of these vaults were deliberately chosen in order to emphasize an upward–soaring quality of line, rather than the downward gravitational one common to many domed structures. . . . The bands of skylights, which separate and articulate the four vaults, increase the sense of airiness and lightness.[45]

Saarinen had come to know techniques of automobile design while working on the General Motors Technical Center, and he now put those techniques into play, shaping and studying the complex shapes of his building in models and using those models as a generator of drawings that followed.[46] Such methods of architectural design became more commonplace in the computer age that followed, but in an era that preceded computer-aided design they were seen as a radically different approach. Detailed photographs of the models not only facilitated study of the design, but also provided key images for presentations to the client (see 15.011–15.014).

With the TWA Terminal, Saarinen joined a small group of architects exploring similarly expressionistic forms at the time. These included Felix Candela, as in his Church of the Miraculous Virgin Mary (Mexico City, 1954), and Enrico Castiglioni, as in his competition entry for the pilgrimage church of the 'Madonna delle Lacrime' (Syracuse, Sicily, 1957). Jørn Utzon's acclaimed design for the Sydney Opera House parallels TWA more closely; Saarinen had been a member of the jury that awarded Utzon first prize in 1957, voicing his support to the other

jurors with drawings of his own that helped to clarify Utzon's concept.[47] The Lambert Airport Terminal in Saint Louis, by Yamasaki, Leinweber, and Associates, also utilizes concrete vaults; it had been completed in 1956, and while more conventionally shaped, it would have provided a viable point of departure for Saarinen's daring exploration of form.

In arriving at his own, more individual solution for TWA, Saarinen may have been influenced, consciously or not, by early examples of modern architecture that had fallen into obscurity, as earlier noted. Given the architecturally charged atmosphere of his youth, it seems likely that he would have known of such books as Platz's *Die Baukunst der neuesten Zeit* (1927). A broad, largely pictorial survey of early twentieth-century architecture unbound by theoretical constraints, it included not only such modern landmarks as buildings by Frank Lloyd Wright, Walter Gropius, and Le Corbusier, but also expressionist designs by Bruno Taut, Hans Poelzig, and Erich Mendelsohn.[48] Otto Bartning's Sternkirche (00.010) would have been particularly appealing. Even closer is Dominikus Bohm's War Memorial Church (New Ulm, Germany, 1928; 00.011), which is astonishingly similar to Saarinen's column studies for TWA (see, for example, 15.015–15.017). It had been published in a similarly inclusive book, Cheney's *New World Architecture*,[49] which included work by Eliel Saarinen. Cheney had visited Eliel Saarinen at Cranbrook while completing his survey, and the younger Saarinen must at least have looked at its illustrations.[50]

Saarinen explored a quite different building technology in his design for the Samuel F. B. Morse and Ezra Stiles Colleges at Yale University (New Haven, Connecticut, 1958–62; 17.001–17.018). Seeking to relate to both the material and vocabulary of Yale's Gothic-revival colleges (then only a few decades old), and further to find a rational means of building the individually-shaped rooms he felt essential to college life, he revived a building technique known as poured stone. Load-bearing walls could be erected economically by first placing stones within wooden formwork, then filling the gaps with concrete to achieve structural rigidity. No skilled masons were required, as Frank Lloyd Wright had known when he revived the technique at Taliesin West beginning in 1938, and the forms themselves could be freely shaped without compromise of structural integrity, somewhat in the manner of an irregular ceramic vessel. In describing his concept, Saarinen had said,

> the rooms should be as individual as possible, as random as those in an old inn rather than as standardized as those in a modern motel. . . . these very special problems could not be solved within the general current vocabulary of modern architecture. . . . An architecture of rectangles and cubes seemed ill-suited, too, to the site. . . . We have made the

00.010. Sternkirche model, 1921, unbuilt; Otto Bartning.
From Gustav Adolf Platz, *Die Baukunst der neuesten Zeit* (Berlin: Propylaen-Verlag, 1927). (ppmsca-17406)

00.011. Swabian Soldiers' Memorial Church, Neu-Ulm, Germany, addition, 1926; Domenikus Böhm, interior.
From Sheldon Cheney, *The New World Architecture* (London, New York, and Toronto: Longmans, Green, 1930). (ppmsca-17408)

buildings polygonal—their shapes derived in order to provide the special and diverse student rooms, to answer the needs of the site and to give variety and sequence of spatial experiences in the court. . . . most significantly, we conceived of these colleges as citadels of earthy, monolithic masonry. . . . masonry walls made without masons, masonry walls which are "modern."[51]

Saarinen's artful arrangement of walls indeed suggested a medieval context, yet without historicizing detail. Sculpture by Constantino Nivola enlivened their massive presence. In concert with the towers of the older campus, Saarinen included a tower as well, its irregular shape not unlike a water tower by Otto Bartning that Platz had included as an example of new architecture (fig. 00.012).

The commission for the Dulles International Airport (Chantilly, Virginia, 1958–63; 18.001–18.036), intended to be seen as a major gateway to the nation's capital, provided Saarinen with a last opportunity to design the sort of monumental structure that he did so well. Like the TWA Terminal, it has become an iconic image of mid-twentieth-century airports, yet it represented a more radical rethinking of the problem. In place of long walkways that so taxed the passenger, Saarinen proposed mobile lounges that would carry the passenger to the plane in comfort and even in style, providing as well for convenient transfers from plane to plane. Such a concept also justified a grand, monumental hall that constituted the working core of the building. Saarinen again exploited suspended structure to define that volume, its cables now attached to dramatically inclined columns. They impart a grand, temple-like appearance to the building, suitable to the image of a national landmark that Saarinen sought, yet one with a greater sense of structural daring than is usual at the Federal level. As Saarinen wrote,

> The tradition of Federal architecture is static, but a jet-age airport should be essentially non-static, expressing the movement and the excitement of travel. We thought that if we could bring these two things together into a unified design we would have a very interesting building.[52]

The building was widely praised; even Temko seemed satisfied: "This is one of the first truly convincing victories of the new architecture in its quest—too often a perversely unconfident quest—for a legitimate monumentalism worthy of a technological age."[53]

Dulles's close resemblance to a sketch by Eric Mendelsohn (00.013) has been much noted, reaffirming Saarinen's link to expressionist designs of the earlier twentieth century. Parallels between Saarinen's later buildings and other expressionistic work of the early twentieth century can also be drawn. For example, the pleated shapes of Saarinen's CBS Tower resemble those of several early, distinctively embellished skyscrapers, as an office building in Dusseldorf (1923–25) by Paul Bonatz (1877–1956) published in Platz.[54] So, too, the central lobby of Saarinen's United States chancellery in Oslo (1955–59) resembles the entrance hall of Peter Behrens's Chemical Factory and Dye Works (Hochst-am-Main, 1920–24).[55] The point is not so much that Saarinen drew from these sources, consciously or subconsciously, but that he broadened modernism in a manner consistent with its earlier beginnings, thus giving modern architecture an expressive voice, a sense of visible purpose and narrative. No wonder Greg Lynn—one of the most promising of a younger generation of American architects exploring similar motifs—recently praised Saarinen's work and spoke of studying the buildings in his travels.[56] Perhaps others will come to acknowledge their debt.

One of Saarinen's last commissions elicited gentle, but no less expressive, results: the North Christian Church in Columbus, Indiana (1959–64; 19.001–19.013). Designed for the same sect as the First Christian Church, but on a more isolated site, it records Saarinen's trajectory from a modernist dedicated to orthodox forms to a modern architect seeking new means of expression. Saarinen's comments regarding the commission could almost be taken as a summary of his noble, career-long quest for meaningful design:

> I don't think religion should be something easy. I think you should have to work for it and it should be a special thing. The architecture should express this. That is an absolutely marvelous experience at Borobudur and Angfor Wat, when you keep climbing those steep steps and all of the time are being subjected by the architecture to awarenesses of special and spiritual qualities.[57]

00.012. Watertower, Zeipau, 1922; Otto Bartning. From Gustav Adolf Platz, *Die Baukunst der neuesten Zeit* (Berlin: Propylaen-Verlag, 1927). (ppmsca-17407)

00.013. Visionary design, ca. 1917; Eric Mendelsohn. From Wolf Von Eckhardt, *Eric Mendelsohn* (New York: George Braziller, 1960). (NA1088.M57 V6)

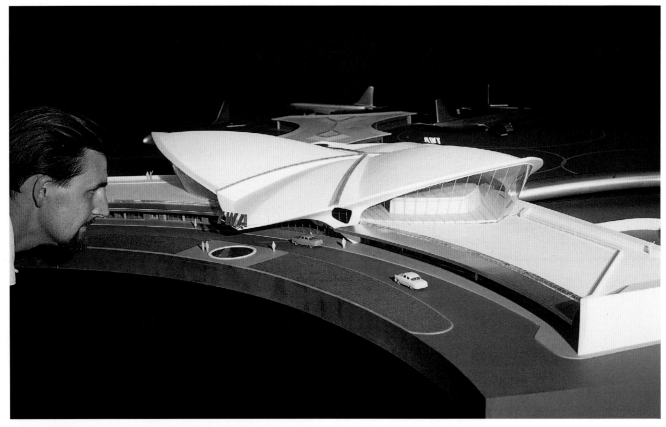

00.014. Balthazar Korab with TWA model. (krb-00012)

BALTHAZAR KORAB:
ARCHITECT AND PHOTOGRAPHER

As an architect who worked in Eero Saarinen's office, Balthazar Korab brings special understanding to the buildings. He knew firsthand of concepts underlying the designs, in some instances helping to develop them, and his photographs record knowing images of Saarinen's intentions.

Korab began his study of architecture in 1945, at the Polytechnicum in Budapest, the city where he had been born in 1926.[58] During the communist uprising of 1949 he left for Paris, where he continued his studies at the Ecole des Beaux-Arts and also, in 1953, worked in Le Corbusier's famed office. Upon receiving his degree in 1955, Korab left for the United States to seek employment with Eero Saarinen, with whom he worked from that year until 1958. To avoid a conflict of interest, he briefly withdrew from Saarinen's office to enter the Sydney Opera House Competition in collaboration with Peter Kollar (1926–2000), a former Budapest classmate. Saarinen was among the judges who awarded them fourth prize in 1957, which, for Kollar (who had emigrated to Australia in 1950), represented the highest award for an Australian architect.[59]

During his years with Saarinen, Korab was actively involved in the design of several projects, including the Miller house in Columbus, Indiana, for which he studied alternate fireplace designs in model form (see 08.031, 08.877–08.882); and the Thomas J. Watson Research Center for IBM, helping to develop the first scheme for that commission (see 13.001, 13.003, 13.016).[60] He also began his career in photography in these years, playing a significant role in Saarinen's use of models both as a means of refining each design and as a basis for presentations to his clients (00.014). As Korab later recalled,

> we developed a way where the camera and its handler became an integral part of the design process. The photograph became a visual test for the designer. We were at times intrigued by the extent Eero grew to depend on those images, particularly during the TWA studies. Both form and space could be conveyed conveniently with my small Leica. Its size allowed access where eyes could not reach and special theatrical effects such as real scenery projected for background and smoke and mirrors were used (literally) to enhance the space impression. Then large scale projection of slides conveyed the "being in it" experience. Finished client presentation with models was eventually replaced by slide shows.[61]

00.015. Hill College House (originally Hill Hall Women's Dormitories), University of Pennsylvania, Philadelphia, 1957–60, model. (krb-00013)

00.016. Hill College House, model. (krb-00014)

00.017. Hill College House, model. (krb-00015)

00.018. Eero Saarinen and Associates office, Bloomfield Hills, Michigan, 1953. (krb-00016)

00.019. Eero Saarinen and Associates office. (krb-00017)

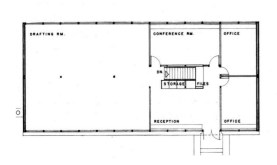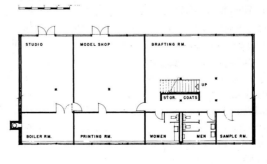

00.020. Office Plans. (ppmsca-15443)

00.021. Eero Saarinen and Associates office, with staff in foreground. (krb-00018)

When Korab spoke of "smoke and mirrors," he indeed meant it; some of the TWA models, for example, were of only half the building, but as the building was symmetrical, a strategically placed mirror, its edges softened by artfully directed lighting, made it seem whole in photographs (see 15.011 for one example).

Gradually photography became a preoccupation, and Korab left Saarinen's office to pursue it as a full-time profession. His insights as architect were now expanded to record work by the major American architects of his time, including Frank Lloyd Wright and Mies van der Rohe, among others. He also photographed anonymous buildings and landscapes, both urban and rural. And he continued to photograph Saarinen's work, too, accumulating an archive of nearly 8,000 images for that architect alone.

This volume comprises images drawn from that archive. Not every building by Saarinen is included, for while Korab photographed most of the work, there are some buildings, such as the Bell Telephone Laboratories (Holmdel, New Jersey, 1957–62), of which he took none

at all. For a few other buildings, the archive might include numerous model shots, as for Hill College House at the University of Pennsylvania (Philadelphia, 1957–60; 00.015–00.017), but only a very few of the completed building itself, and those more in the nature of quick notes than images for publication; these "notes" are not included here. Yet for the buildings that are included, there are usually between 100 and 400 images from which to choose. Some buildings are represented by more than 500 images—as TWA, Dulles (nearly 600), General Motors (over 700) and the Miller house in Columbus (over 1,000). Here the images are grouped by building, and the buildings are arranged in chronological order according to the date of the building's commission. For multiple commissions received in the same year, the buildings are arranged in chronological order according to the date of their individual completion. Additional images of interest are reproduced in an appendix and on the accompanying DVD, suggesting the greater extent of this archive.

SAARINEN OFFICE STAFF

00.022. Edward Saad? (krb-00019).

00.023. Eero Saarinen (left) and Kevin Roche (krb-00020).

00.024. Eero Saarinen (left) and Tom Lucas (krb-00023).

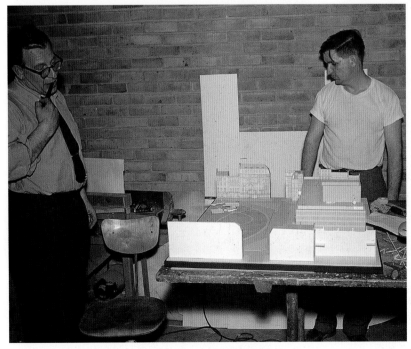

00.025. Eero Saarinen (left) and Alan Tunstall (krb-00022).

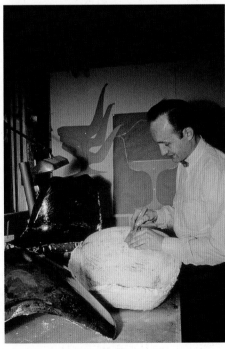

00.026. Don Pettit (krb-00021).

00.027. Saarinen office staff before hirsute enhancement; Eero Saarinen, upper right; Kevin Roche, lower right. (krb-00025)

00.028. . . . and after enhancement. (krb-00026)

00.029. Kevin Roche at Balthazar Korab's house, Birmingham, Michigan (krb-00024).

00.030. Monica Korab, at Balthazar Korab's first studio, Birmingham, Michigan. (krb-00027)

00.031 Eero Saarinen house, Bloomfield Hills, Michigan; alterations, 1947–59. (krb-00028)

Korab also captured less formal, and sometimes unexpected, images of the office and of Saarinen's family. The modest building that Saarinen designed for his own studio rarely figures in discussions of his work (Eero Saarinen and Associates Office, Bloomfield Hills, Michigan, 1953; 00.018, 00.019, and 00.020), but the intense rhythm of work within its walls, and the roster of assistants who went on to distinguished careers of their own, have drawn attention.[62] The atmosphere must have seemed like that of an informal academy, one not unlike Cranbrook itself. Korab recalled that "it was probably the most creative, the most exciting office in the world at that time."[63] Undated photographs show the staff grouped before the building (00.021) and at work within (00.022–00.025). Others record lighter moments that must have relieved long hours of intense labor (00.026–00.029), including a few of the woman who would become Korab's wife and a major assistant in his own photographic studio (00.030).

Saarinen never designed a house for himself, but instead remodeled a dwelling that had been built beween 1860 and 1870 (00.031).[64] It provided an idealized setting for some of Saarinen's well known designs for mass-produced furniture, as the "Womb" chair (No. 70 for Knoll Associates, Inc., 1946–48) and groupings of his "Pedestal"

00.032. Interior, Saarinen House, Bloomfield Hills. (krb-00029)

series (also for Knoll, 1955–57; 00.032). Nearby, Saarinen designed a small home for his mother; after her death, it served as a guest house (00.033 and 00.034). Also within the Korab archive are pictures of Saarinen's extended family (00.035). In a way, Saarinen's dedicated staff must have constituted an even more extended family, working collaboratively in the manner advocated by Eliel Saarinen, yet more connected to the architectural issues of their day.

00.033. Eero Saarinen guest house (originally Loja Saarinen house), Bloomfield Hills, Michigan, 1950–51. (krb-00030)

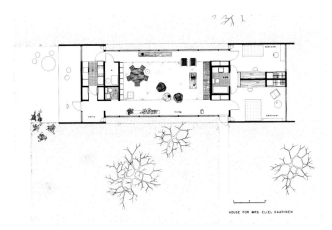

00.034. Eero Saarinen guest house plan. (ppmsca-15442)

00.035. Eero Saarinen family at Cranbrook, August 1958: back row, left to right: Eric Saarinen (son of Eero and Lily Swann Saarinen), Donald Louchheim, Harry Allen Louchheim (sons of Aline Louchheim Saarinen). Front row, left to right: Susan Saarinen (daughter of Eero and Lily Swann Saarinen), Eero Saarinen, Loja Saarinen, Aline Louchheim Saarinen, Eames Saarinen (son of Eero and Aline Louchheim Saarinen).

NOTES

1 Vincent Scully recently spoke of this, as summarized by Jayne Merkel, "Symposium finds Saarinen's reputation back on the upswing," *Architectural Record* (June 2005), not paginated. The symposium in question, "Eero Saarinen: Form-Giver of the 'American Century'," was held at Yale University on April 1–2, 2005, as part of the Saarinen Project of Yale and the Finnish Cultural Institute. For an additional summary of the symposium, see John Harwood, "Giving Form (& Substance) to Eero Saarinen," *Constructs* (Yale University School of Architecture), Fall 2005, 6–9.

2 As discussed in Andrea Dean, "Eero Saarinen in Perspective," *Journal of the American Institute of Architects* 70 (November 1981), 36–51. Jayne Merkel also mentioned this in an interview with Paul Makovsky, "Reconsidering Eero," *Metropolis* (October 2005), 134–139.

3 Allan Temko, *Eero Saarinen* (New York: George Braziller, 1962), 36–37, 41. The buildings in question were IBM Rochester and Deere and Company.

4 Peter Papademetriou, "Coming of Age: Eero Saarinen and Modern American Architecture," *Perspecta* (Yale School of Architecture Journal) no. 21 (1984), 116–43.

5 The concept of style as a matter of personal choice arose with the rise of the Picturesque point of view during the late eighteenth and early nineteenth centuries; the basic text on the Picturesque is Christopher Hussey, *The Picturesque; Studies in a Point of View* (1927; reprinted, Hamden, Connecticut: Archon Books, 1967.

6 Meyer Shapiro, " Style," in *Anthropology today: An Encyclopedic Inventory* (Chicago: University of Chicago Press, 1953), 287–312; reprinted in Meyer Shapiro, *Theory and Philosophy of Art: Style, Artist, and Society* (New York: George Braziller, 1994), 51–102.

7 Sarah Williams Goldhagen, "Something to Talk About; Modernism, Discourse, Style," *Journal of the Society of Architectural Historians* 64 (June 2005), 144–67.

8 Among the most accessible of the early publications, Henry-Russell Hitchcock and Philip Johnson, *The International Style* (1932; reprinted, New York: W. W. Norton, 1966). By 1970, Hitchcock and Johnson, looking back, were amazed that their definition of a particular vocabulary had had such effect, as I learned while studying with Professor Hitchcock in the 1970s. Johnson's own architectural diversity in later years spoke even more strongly of his refusal to be constrained by his curatorial conclusions of 1932.

9 Eero Saarinen, 1958, as quoted in Aline Saarinen, editor, *Eero Saarinen on His Work* (New Haven and London: Yale University Press, 1968), 6.

10 Eero Saarinen, as quoted in Aline Saarinen, 11.

11 Eero Saarinen, as quoted in Aline Saarinen, 16.

12 As I discuss in *Louis I. Kahn: In the Realm of Architecture* (co-authored with David B. Brownlee; New York: Rizzoli, 1991), 50–73. Kahn described modern architecture of his day as "tinny" in 1950 and wrote of his frustration with the open plan in 1958 and 1959; 50 and 56.

13 Robert Venturi, *Complexity and Contradiction in Architecture* (New York: The Museum of Modern Art, 1966), 25. The manuscript for this book was completed in 1963, as I discovered when visiting Venturi's office that year..

14 Eero Saarinen, as quoted in Aline Saarinen, 5–6.

15 Biographical information on the Saarinens, including examples of Eero Saarinen's early work, are included in my essay, "Eliel Saarinen and the Cranbrook Tradition in Architecture and Urban Design," *Design in America; The Cranbrook Vision, 1925–1950* (New York:

Harry N. Abrams in association with the Detroit Institute of Arts and the Metropolitan Museum of Art, 1983), 46–89. Additional biographical information is found in the appendix of that book. For examples of Eero Saarinen's early work, Peter C. Papademetriou, "On Becoming a Modern Architect: Eero Saarinen's Early Work 1928–1948," Oz (Kansas State University) 9 (1987), 56–63.

16 I examined these drawings in the archive of the Suomen Rakennustaiteen Museo in Helsinki in 1981.

17 Eero Saarinen to Florence Shust, ca. 1935, in the possession of Florence Shust Knoll Bassett. I am grateful to R. Craig Miller for bringing this correspondence to my attention in 1981. Florence Shust was among the first graduates of the Kingswood School for Girls and a close friend of the Saarinens, as discussed in Jayne Merkel, Eero Saarinen (New York and London: Phaidon Press, 2005), 37.

18 According to my interview with Ralph Rapson in December, 1981.

19 For additional discussion of this and related projects, De Long, "Eliel Saarinen and the Cranbrook Tradition," 68–72.

20 Saarinen's work with Bel Geddes is cited in Papademetriou, 59. Eero had worked for the Office of Strategic Services in Washington during the war, but returned to Bloomfield Hills in 1945 to rejoin his father.

21 De Long, "Eliel Saarinen and the Cranbrook Tradition," 72.

22 Eero Saarinen, as quoted in Aline Saarinn, 30.

23 Eero Saarinen, as quoted in Aline Saarinen, 32.

24 For example, Antonio Roman, Eero Saarinen; An Architecture of Multiplicity (New York: Princeton University Press, 2003), 168–169; and Papademetriou, "Coming of Age," 131.

25 Frank Lloyd Wright, "The Art and Craft of the Machine" (1901), reprinted, Frank Lloyd Wright, Collected Writings, edited by Bruce Brooks Pfeiffer (New York: Rizzoli in association with the Frank Lloyd Wright Foundation, 1992), vol. I, 58–69. In conversations with Balthazar Korab in July, 2005, he recalled that the circular stair had been detailed by Kevin Roche.

26 Eero Saarinen, as quoted in Aline Saarinen, 22

27 As Kahn expressed to his students at the University of Pennsylvania in the fall of 1962; I was a student in the class at the time.

28 Among many publications on the architecture of Columbus, Columbus Indiana: A Look at the Architecture (Columbus, Indiana: Columbus Area Chamber of Commerce, Inc., 1974).

29 The area is described in Denny Lee, "The Malibu of the North," The New York Times (September 16, 2005), F1, F5.

30 As recounted in "The Maturing Modern," Time 68 (July 2, 1956), 50–57. For additional discussion of the form, Saarinen as quoted in Aline Saarinen, 40.

31 As recorded by docuents in the MIT Museum archive, the consulting firm of Bolt, Beranek, and Newman, all on the MIT faculty.

32 Eero Saarinen, as quoted in Aline Saarinen, 42.

33 Eero Saarinen, as quoted in Aline Saarinen, 48.

34 With Ray Eames's assistance, I examined these drawings in 1981. Case Study House No. 9 was completed for John Entenza in 1950; Case Study No. 8 was completely redesigned by Charles and Ray Eames in 1948 and completed in 1949 for their own house. Among publications on the Case Study houses, Blueprints for Modern Living: History and Legacy of the Case Study Houses (Los Angeles: The Museum of Contemporary Art, 1989). For a discussion of Saarinen's collaboration on these projects, Peter Papademetriou, "Eames, Saarinen: A Magic Box," Casabella 62 (1998/1999), 120–33.

35 Eero Saarinen, as quoted in Aline Saarinen, 56.

36 Eero Saarinen, as quoted in Aline Saarinen, 56.

37 Allan Temko, Eero Saarinen (New York: George Braziller, 1962),

36–37.

38 For an extended discussion of these, see Merkel, especially 85.

39 Eero Saarinen, as quoted in Aline Saarinen, 76, 80.

40 Temko, 41.

41 Eero Saarinen, as quoted in Aline Saarinen, 60.

42 Eero Saarinen, as quoted in Aline Saarinen, 11.

43 Vincent Scully, American Architecture and Urbanism (New York and Washington, Frederick A. Praeger, 1969), 198.

44 Edgar Kaufmann, jr., "Inside Eero Saarinen's TWA Building," Interiors 121 (July 1962), 86–93.

45 Eero Saarinen, as quoted in Aline Saarinen, 68. Reportedly the airline's president, Ralph Dawson, had been similarly inclined toward a building that expressed flight; Merkel, 205.

46 Harry Weese, who had studied with Eero Saarinen at Cranbrook, spoke of how Saarinen was influenced by automobile designers, as recounted in Andrea Dean, "Eero Saarinen in Perspective," Journal of the American Institute of Architects 70 (November 1981), 36–[51].

47 As described in "Breakdown at Sydney," Builder 192 (March 1, 1957), 397–407, and more recently in Geraldine Brooks, "Unfinished Business; Jørn Utzon returns to the Sydney Opera House," The New Yorker (October 17, 2005), 96–111. After innumerable delays during construction, the Opera House opened in 1973. Relationships between TWA and Sydney are explored in Antonio Roman, Eero Saarinen, 187, 190–91.

48 Gustav Adolf Platz, Die Baukunst der neuesten Zeit (Berlin: Propylaen-Verlag, 1927).

49 Sheldon Cheney, The New World Architecture (London, New York, and Toronto: Longmans, Green and Co., 1930).

50 Letter, Sheldon Cheney to George Booth, January 12, 1930, requesting a meeting with Eliel Saarinen; Cranbrook Archives. Saarinen is thanked for his time in the introduction to the book, vii.

51 Eero Saarinen, as quoted in Aline Saarinen, 88, 92.

52 Eero Saarinen, as quoted in Aline Saarinen, 102.

53 Temko, 115–16.

54 Platz, 358.

55 Among several illustrations of Behren's hall lobby is Arnold Whittick, European Architecture in the Twentieth Century (London: Lockwood & Son, 1950), vol. I, plate LXX.

56 As noted by Bryan Fuermann, "Giving Form (& Substance) to Eero Saarinen," 8. I am grateful to Peter Eisenman for first bringing Lynn's talent to my attention.

57 Eero Saarinen as quoted in Aline Saarinen, 96.

58 Biographical information is drawn from Balthazar Korab's curriculum vitae and from biographical portraits, such as that by Kristie Everett Zamora, "Balthazar Korab, Photographer," a brochure accompanying an exhibition at the Flint [Michigan] Institute of Arts, September 13–November 18, 2001.

59 As summarized in Katie Bird, "Associate Professor Laslo Kollar," Origins (Newsletter of the UNSW Archives) 9 (May 2005), 6–7.

60 As Korab related to me during interviews in July, 2005.

61 Balthazar Korab, "Remembering Eero Saarinen; The Bloomfield Hills Office, 1955–58," typed manuscript, ca. 2000 (the full text is published on pages 410–11).

62 For example, Nancy Lickerman Halik, "The Eero Saarinen Spawn," Inland Architect (May 1981), 14–45, as cited in Merkel, note 28, 246. Also, Steven Litt, "Saarinen Fest at Cranbrook," Progressive Architecture 76 (October 1995), 37–38.

63 Balthazar Korab, as quoted in Litt, 38.

64 As recalled by Korab during interviews in July 2005.

BUILDINGS

01 GENERAL MOTORS TECHNICAL CENTER

Warren, Michigan, 1945, 1946–56

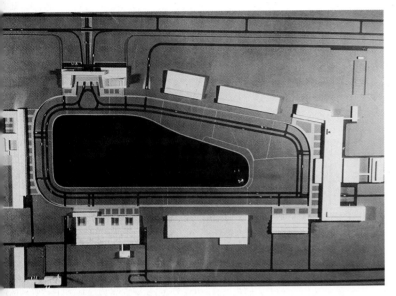

01.001

01.002

01.001. Model (krb-00044).

01.002. General Motors Technical Center. (krb-00048)

01.003. Aerial view. (krb-00047)

01.004. Dome, Styling. (krb-00060) ➤➤

01.003

01.005. Dome, view from
Styling. (krb-00052)

01.006. Dome, view from
Styling. (krb-00053)

01.006

01.007

01.007. Styling. (krb-00113)

01.008. Dome, view from
Styling. (krb-00114)

01.008

01.009. Styling and Dome. (krb-00051)

01.010. Dome, view from water tower.
(krb-00057)

01.009

01.011. Water tower. (krb-00069)

01.012. Water tower, view from
island. (krb-00064)

01.011

01.013. Water tower. (krb-00066)
01.014. Water tower. (krb-00067)

01.013   01.014

01.015. Fountains. (krb-00076) ➤➤   01.019. Fountains. (krb-00074) ➤➤
01.016. Fountains. (krb-00079) ➤➤   01.020. Fountains. (krb-00073) ➤➤
01.017. Fountains. (krb-00080) ➤➤   01.021. Fountains. (krb-00072) ➤➤
01.018. Fountains. (krb-00081) ➤➤

01.015

01.016

01.017

01.018

01.019

01.020

01.021

01.022

01.023

01.024

01.025

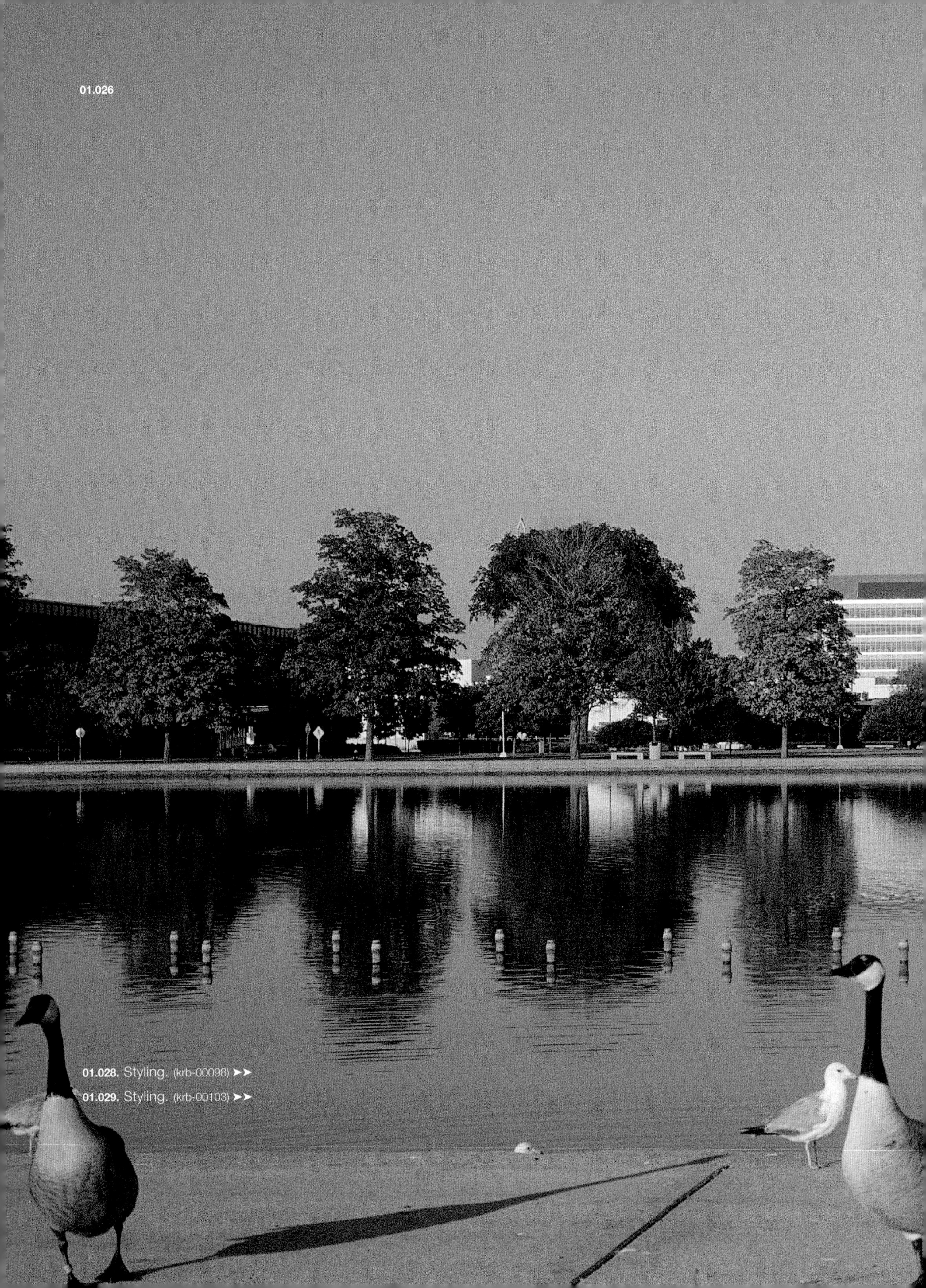

01.028. Styling. (krb-00098) ➤➤
01.029. Styling. (krb-00103) ➤➤

01.027

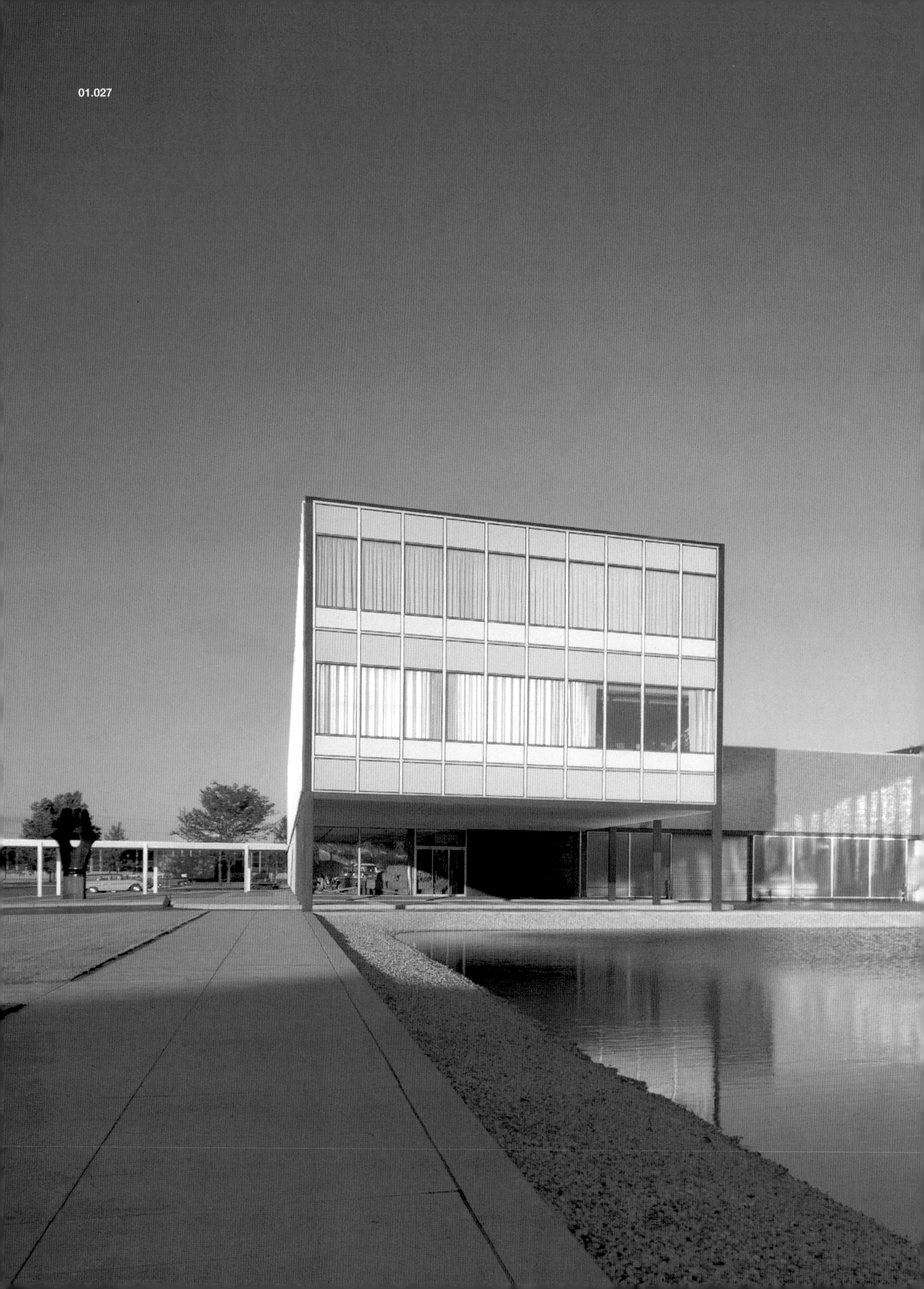

01.028

01.029

01.030. Styling. (krb-00110)
01.031. Service Section. (krb-00111)
01.032. Styling. (krb-00109)

01.030

01.031

01.032

01.033. Research. (krb-00117)
01.034. Research. (krb-00115)

01.033

01.034

01.035. Service Section. (krb-00105)

01.036. Unidentified. (krb-00097)

01.037. Service Section. (krb-00093)

01.038. Engineering. (krb-00090)

01.035

01.036

01.037

01.038

01.039

01.039. Research.
(krb-00120)

01.040. Research cafeteria interior detail.
(krb-00124)

01.041. Engineering.
(krb-00123)

01.040

01.041

01.042

01.042. Research.
(krb-00126)

01.043. Dynamometer
Building. (krb-00125)

01.044. Dynamometer
Building. (krb-00127)

01.043

01.044

01.045

01.045. Research. (krb-00094)
01.046. Research. (krb-00096)
01.047. Research. (krb-00095)

01.046

01.047

01.048. Styling. (krb-00099)
01.049. Research. (krb-00102)

01.048

01.049

01.050. Research. (krb-00121)

01.051. Process Development.
(krb-00119)

01.052. Unidentified. (krb-00122)

01.050

01.051

01.052

01.053. Styling Administration interior.
(krb-00137)

01.054. Styling Administration interior.
(krb-00138)

01.055. Styling Administration interior,
restored. (krb-00139)

01.053

01.054

01.055

01.056. Styling Administration
interior, restored. (krb-00134)

01.057. Styling Administration
interior, restored. (krb-00135)

01.056

01.057

01.058

01.058. Styling Administration, stair. (krb-00142)

01.059. Styling Administration, stair. (krb-00143)

01.060. Styling Administration, stair. (krb-00141)

01.059

01.060

01.061. Research,
model for stair.
(krb-00145)

01.062. Research
Administration, interior.
(krb-00147)

01.063. Research
Administration, stair.
(krb-00146) ➤➤

01.061

01.062

01.064. Research Administration, stair. (krb-00149)

01.065. Research Administration, stair. (krb-00148)

01.064

01.065

01.067

01.068

02 SAINT LOUIS GATEWAY ARCH

St. Louis, Missouri, 1947–65

02.001

02.002

02.001. Model. (krb-00158)

02.002. Model. (krb-00157)

02.003. View across Mississippi.
(krb-00153)

02.003

02.004

02.004. Construction. (krb-00163)

02.005. Mockup for stair with Eero Saarinen at Bloomfield Hills office. (krb-00162)

02.006. View from park. (krb-00177)

02.005

02.006

02.007. View from old cathedral.
(krb-00167)

02.008. View from old St. Louis
Courthouse. (krb-00165)

02.007

02.008

02.009. View.
(krb-00178)

02.010. View from
park. (krb-00181)

02.011. View.
(krb-00179) ➤➤

02.010

02.012. View. (krb-00184)

02.013. View from park
at dawn. (krb-00175)

02.012

02.013

02.014. View from old cathedral at dusk. (krb-00168)

02.015. View at dusk. (krb-00173)

02.016. View toward bridge at dusk. (krb-00174)

02.017. View at dusk.
(krb-00164) ➤➤

02.014

02.015

02.016

02.017

03 MILLER HOUSE

Ontario, Canada, 1950–52

03.001

03.002

03.001. View from lake. (krb-00186)

03.002. View from lake. (krb-00190)

03.003. View from east. (krb-00191)

03.004. View from terrace.
(krb-00197) ➤➤

03.003

03.005. Terrace. (krb-00194)

03.006. Terrace dining area. (krb-00199)

03.007. Terrace. (krb-00196)

03.005

03.006

03.007

03.008. View from terrace.
(krb-00198)

03.009. Entrance. (krb-00204)

03.010. Entrance from terrace
dining area. (krb-00203)

03.008

03.009

03.010

03.011. Terrace dining area. (krb-00201)

03.012. Terraced area. (krb-00207)

03.013. View toward lake from dining area. (krb-00200)

03.011

03.012

03.014. Dining room. (krb-00211) ➤➤

03.015. Bedroom. (krb-00214) ➤➤

03.016. Living area. (krb-00208) ➤➤

03.017. Living area at dusk. (krb-00209) ➤➤

03.018. View from terrace at dusk. (krb-00202) ➤➤

03.013

03.014

03.015

03.016

04 IRWIN UNION BANK & TRUST COMPANY

Columbus, Indiana, 1950–54

04.001

04.002

04.001. View from park.
(krb-00218)

04.002. View from street.
(krb-00220)

04.003. View from street.
(krb-00219)

04.003

04.004. Aerial view. (krb-00222)

04.005. Aerial view. (krb-00223)

04.006. Aerial view. (krb-00221)

04.004

04.005

04.007. Main floor, interior.
(krb-00232) ➤➤

04.008. Main floor, interior.
(krb-00229) ➤➤

04.006

04.009. Main floor, interior. (krb-00231)

04.010. Main floor, interior. (krb-00234)

04.011. Main floor, interior. (krb-00233)

04.009

04.010

04.012. Stair to lower level. (krb-00235) ➤➤

04.013. Main floor at dusk. (krb-00228) ➤➤

04.014. View from park at dusk.
(krb-00227) ➤➤

04.011

04.013

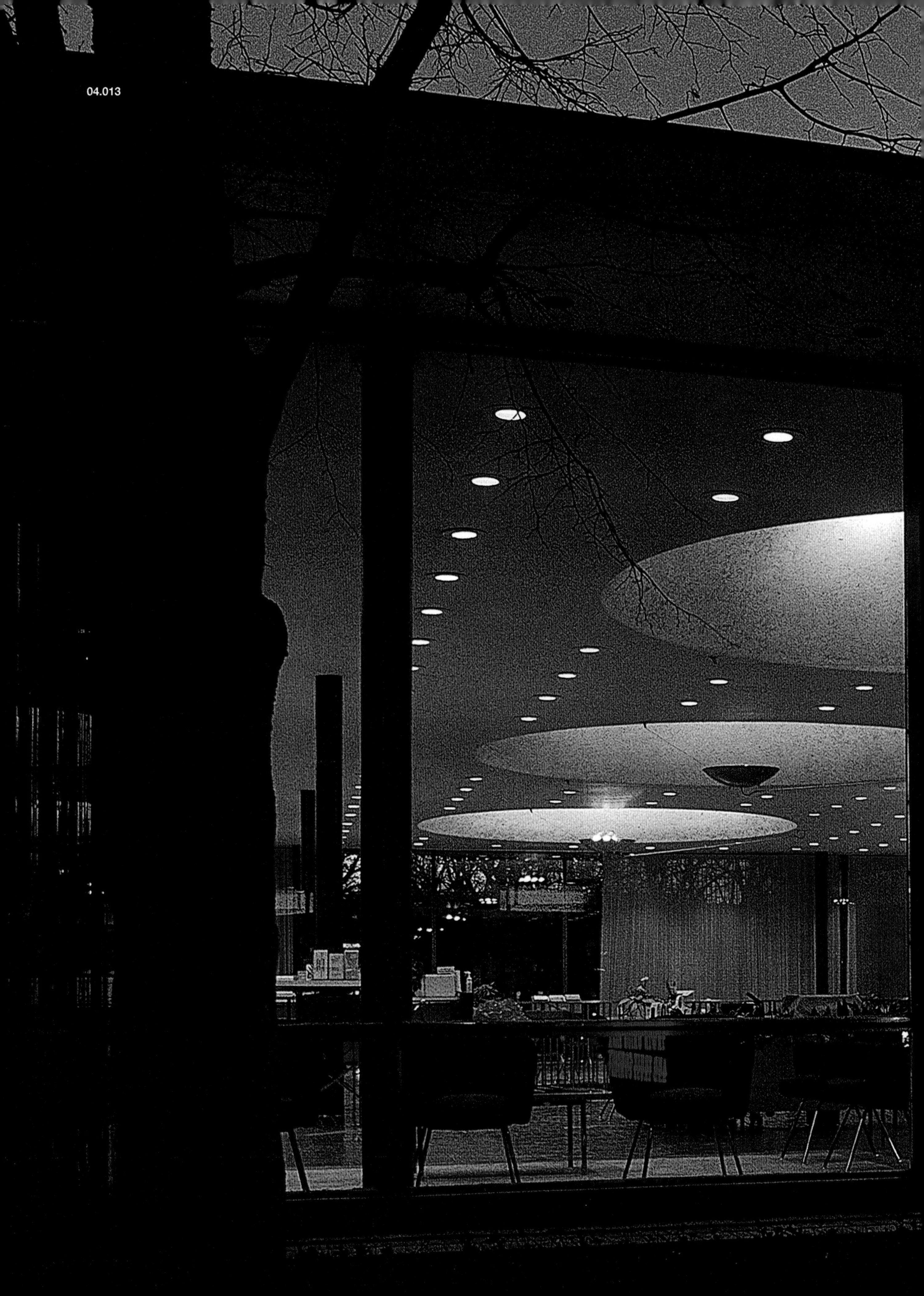

05 MIT

KRESGE AUDITORIUM AND CHAPEL

Cambridge, Massachusetts, 1950–55

05.001

05.002

05.001. Model. (krb-00237)

05.002. Aerial view. (krb-00238)

05.003. Auditorium. (krb-00239)

05.004. Auditorium and chapel. (krb-00241) ➤➤

05.003

05.004

05.005. Auditorium. (krb-00244)

05.006. Auditorium and chapel.
(krb-00242)

05.005

05.007. Auditorium lobby. (krb-00246)

05.008. Auditorium. (krb-00247)

05.009. Auditorium, interior.
(krb-00252) ➤➤

05.010. Auditorium, interior.
(krb-00249) ➤➤

05.011. Auditorium, interior.
(krb-00250) ➤➤

05.012. Auditorium. (krb-00248) ➤➤

05.007

05.008

05.009

05.010

05.012

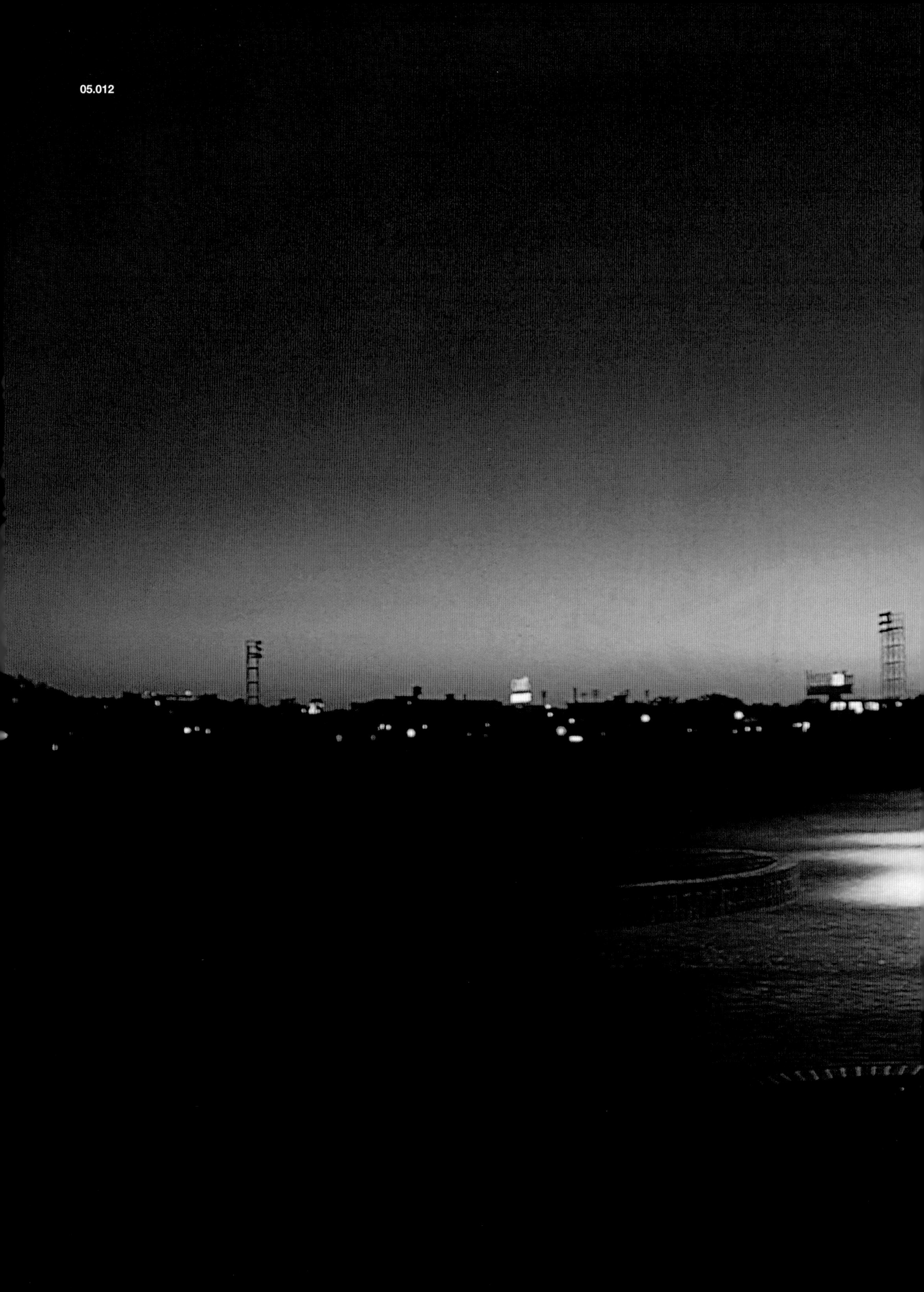

05.013

05.014

05.013. Chapel. (krb-00257)

05.014. Auditorium and chapel.
(krb-00255)

05.015. Chapel. (krb-00254)

05.015

05.016. Chapel entrance. (krb-00256)
05.017. Chapel moat. (krb-00258)
05.018. Chapel detail. (krb-00259)

05.017

05.018

05.016

05.019

05.020

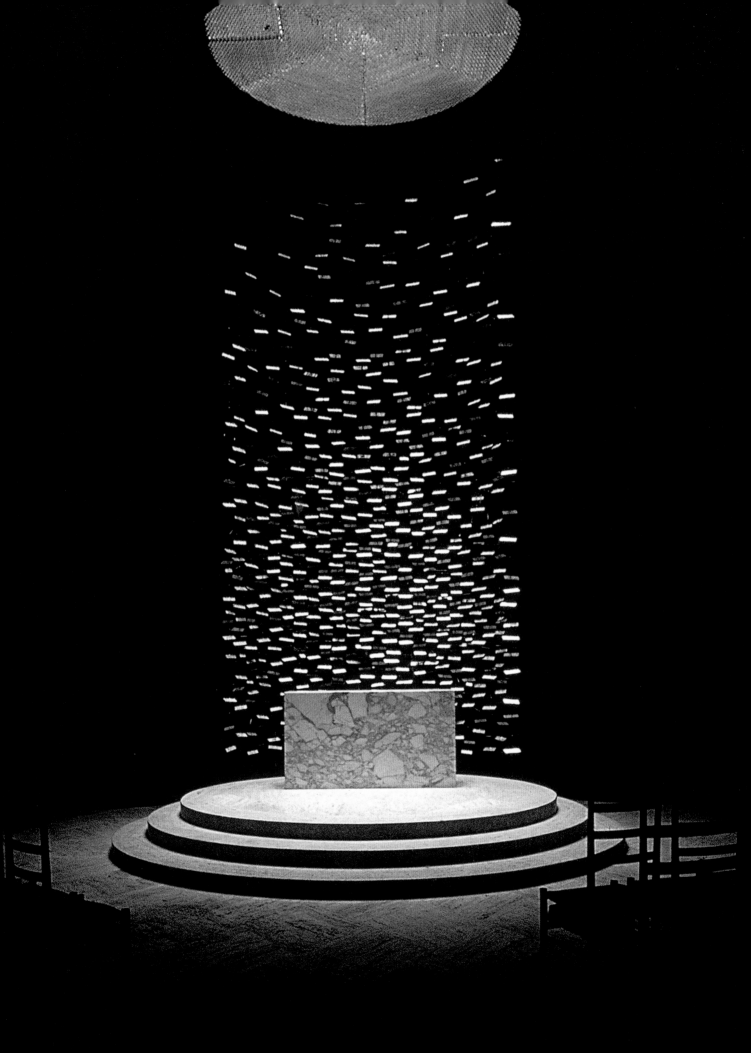

06 MILWAUKEE ART MUSEUM

Milwaukee, Wisconsin, 1952–57

06.001

06.002

06.001. View. (krb-00265)

06.002. View with mosaic.
(krb-00269)

06.003. View. (krb-00267)

06.004. View. (krb-00264) ➤➤

06.003

06.005

06.005. View toward Lake Michigan.
(krb-00272)

06.006. View toward Lake Michigan.
(krb-000274)

06.007. View from below. (krb-00270)

06.006

06.007

06.008. View from below. (krb-00271) ➤➤

06.009. View toward Lake Michigan. (krb-00273) ➤➤

06.009

06.010. View from below. (krb-00263)

06.011. Courtyard. (krb-00820)

06.012. Courtyard, view toward
Lake Michigan. (krb-00276) ➤➤

06.010

06.011

06.013

06.013. Interior stair.
(krb-00277)

06.014. Exterior stair.
(krb-00278)

06.015. Interior stair.
(krb-00279)

06.014

06.015

07 UNIVERSITY OF MICHIGAN

SCHOOL OF MUSIC

Ann Arbor, Michigan, 1952–56

07.001

07.002

07.001. Model. (krb-00287)

07.002. Model. (krb-00290)

07.003. View from lake. (krb-00282)

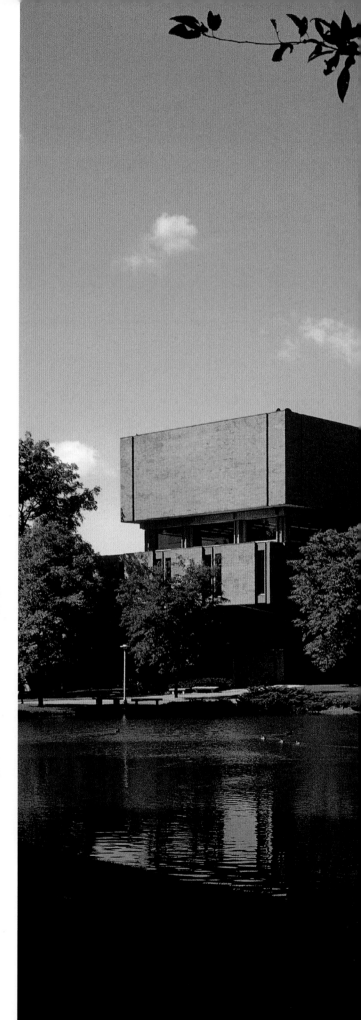

07.003

07.004. Model. (krb-00283)
07.005. Aerial view. (krb-00293)

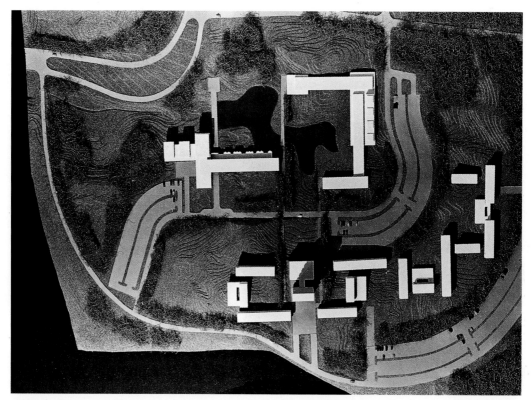

07.004

07.005

07.006. Model. (krb-00285)
07.007. Model. (krb-00289)

07.006

07.007

07.008. View. (krb-00280) ➤➤

07.009

07.009. View. (krb-00306)
07.010. Entrance. (krb-00302)
07.011. View. (krb-00307)

07.010

07.011

08 MILLER HOUSE

Columbus, Indiana, 1953–57

08.001

08.001. Aerial view. (krb-00319)

08.002. View from pool. (krb-00329)

08.003. View from river. (krb-00327) ➤➤

08.002

08.003

08.004. Garden pool.
(krb-00325)

08.005. View from terrace.
(krb-00345)

08.006. View from garden.
(krb-00331) ➤➤

08.004

08.005

08.007. View from garden. (krb-00336)
08.008. Garden. (krb-00333)
08.009. Terrace. (krb-00312)

08.007

08.008

08.009

08.010. Garden. (krb-00397)
08.011. Garden. (krb-00393)

08.010

08.011

08.012. Garden. (krb-00402)

08.013. Garden. (krb-00408)

08.012

08.013

08.014. Garden. (krb-00406)
08.015. Garden. (krb-00396)
08.016. Garden. (krb-00410)

08.014

08.015

08.017. Garden. (krb-00411) ➤➤
08.018. Garden. (krb-00407) ➤➤
08.019. Terrace. (krb-00346) ➤➤

08.016

08.017

08.018

08.020. Terrace. (krb-00338)

08.021. Column detail. (krb-00339)

08.022. Terrace. (krb-00334)

08.020

08.021

08.022

08.023. Entrance. (krb-00348)

08.024. Entrance, interior. (krb-00374)

08.025. Living area. (krb-00350) ➤➤

08.024

08.026. Living area. (krb-00352)
08.027. Living area. (krb-00351)

08.026

08.027

08.029

08.028. Living area. (krb-00355)

08.029. Living area. (krb-00359)

08.031

08.032

08.030. Living area. (krb-00370)

08.031. Study model for
fireplace. (krb-00367)

08.032. Living area, fireplace.
(krb-00372)

08.033. Dining area. (krb-00377)

08.034. Dining area. (krb-00378)

08.035. Living area with dining table in foreground. (krb-00379)

08.033

08.034

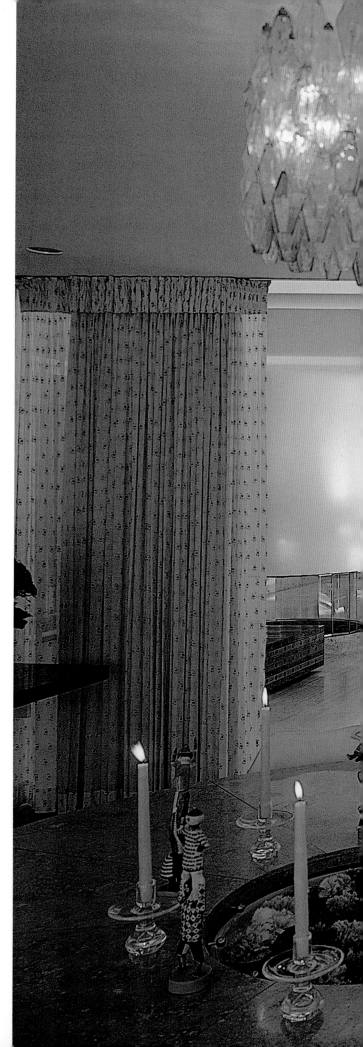

08.035

08.037

08.038

08.036. Children's area.
(krb-00382)

08.037. Dining area details.
(krb-00381)

08.038. Bathroom. (krb-00387)

08.039. Recreation area.
(krb-00384) ➤➤

08.040. View at dusk.
(krb-00314) ➤➤

08.039

08.040

09 CONCORDIA
THEOLOGICAL SEMINARY

Fort Wayne, Indiana, 1953–58

09.001

09.001. Model. (krb-00419)

09.002. Chapel from entrance
court. (krb-00418)

09.002

09.003. Chapel entrance. (krb-00415)

09.004. Chapel, belfry, and dining hall. (krb-00421)

09.004

09.005. Distant view. (krb-00414) ➤➤

09.006

09.006. Administration, dining hall, belfry and chapel. (krb-00420)

09.007. Administration and chapel from lake. (krb-00416)

09.008. Chapel, commons and dining hall. (krb-00423)

09.007

09.008

09.009. Chapel, interior. (krb-00425)
09.010. Chapel, interior. (krb-00427)
09.011. Chapel, interior. (krb-00424)

09.009

09.010

09.011

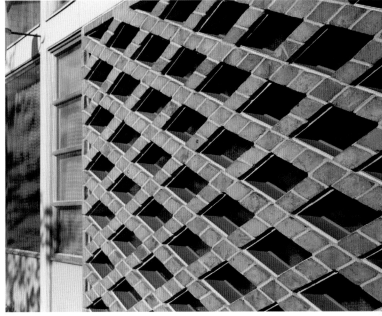

09.012. Commons, interior.
(krb-00432)

09.013. Commons, brickwork
detail. (krb-00433)

09.014. View at dusk.
(krb-00413) ➤➤

10 UNIVERSITY OF CHICAGO
LAW SCHOOL

Chicago, Illinois, 1955–60

10.001

10.001. Library. (krb-00439)

10.002. Administration building and library. (krb-00440)

10.002

10.004

10.005

10.003. Library with administration building and moot court in foreground. (krb-00438)

10.004. Library. (krb-00442)

10.005. Administration building and library. (krb-00443)

10.006. Administration building and library. (krb-00444) ▶▶

10.006

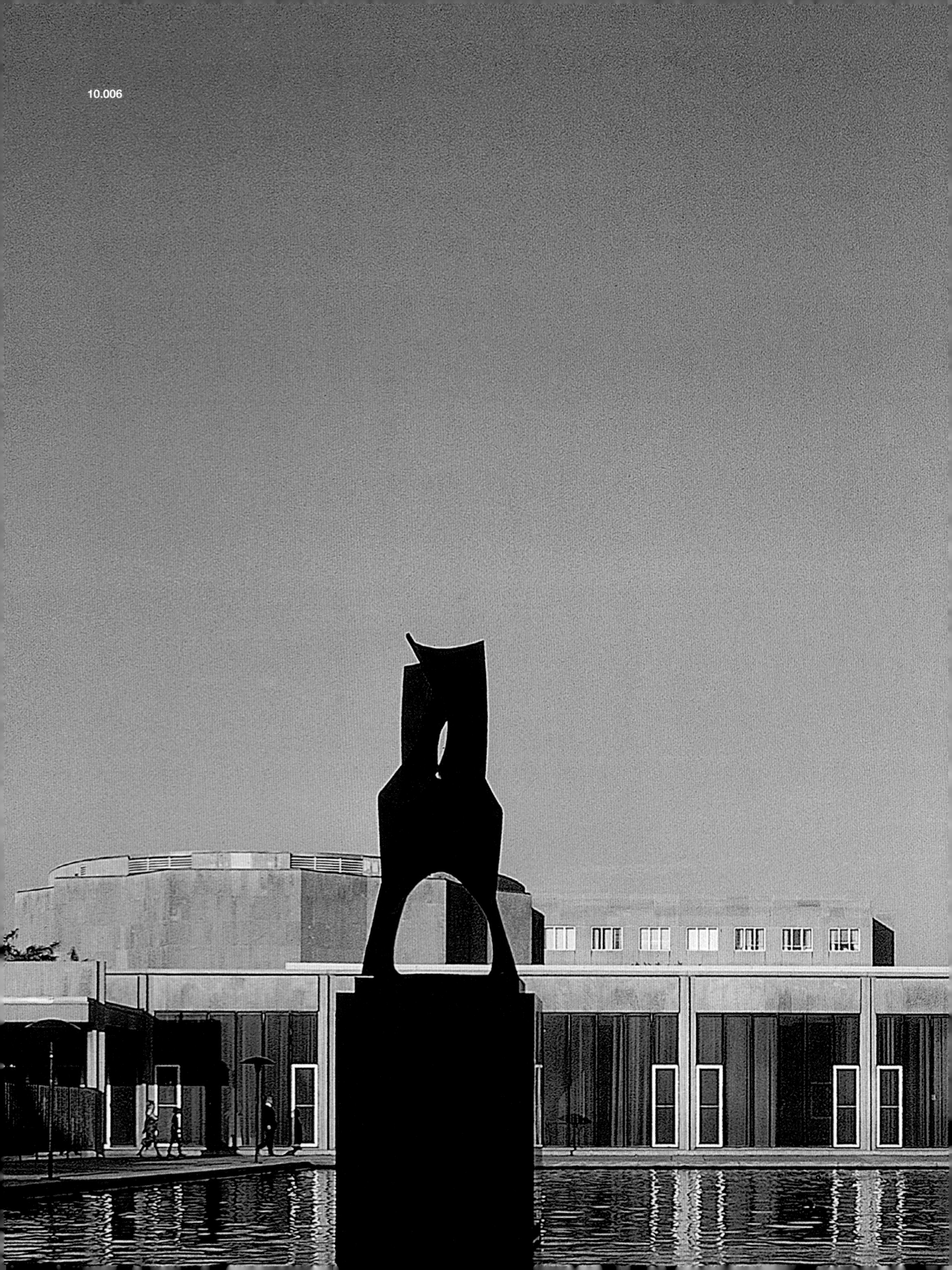

11 UNITED STATES CHANCELLERY

London, 1955–60

11.001

11.002

11.001. Model. (krb-00453)

11.002. Model. (krb-00450)

11.003. View from Grosvenor
Square. (krb-00447)

11.003

236

11.004. East front detail. (krb-00458)

11.005. East front. (krb-00457)

11.006. East front. (krb-00459)

11.004

11.005

11.007. Wall detail. (krb-00464) ➤➤

11.008. Corner detail. (krb-00460) ➤➤

11.006

11.007

11.009. Corner detail.
(krb-00465)

11.010. Rear view.
(krb-00466)

11.0010

11.011. Rear court. (krb-00469)

11.012. View from lobby. (krb-00471)

11.011

11.012

244 UNITED STATES CHANCELLERY

11.013

11.014

11.015

11.016

11.015. Library. (krb-00473)

11.016. Office. (krb-00475)

11.017. Office area. (krb-00474) ➤➤

11.017

11.018. Auditorium. (krb-00477)
11.019. Auditorium. (krb-00475)

11.018

11.019

11.021

11.020. View at dusk. (krb-00448)
11.021. View at dusk. (krb-00446)

12 IBM
MANUFACTURING AND TRAINING FACILITY

Rochester, Minnesota, 1956–58

12.001

12.002

12.001. Model. (krb-00488)

12.002. Aerial view. (krb-00490)

12.003. View. (krb-00480)

12.004. View. (krb-00479) ➤➤

12.003

12.005. View. (krb-00481)
12.006. Wall detail. (krb-00505)

12.005

12.007

12.008

12.009

12.010

12.011

12.007. Wall studies. (krb-00483)

12.008. Wall studies with with Kevin Roche, Aline Saarinen, and Eero Saarinen. (krb-00486)

12.009. Wall studies with Balthazar Korab and unidentified staff member. (krb-00484)

12.010. Wall studies. (krb-00482)

12.011. Wall mockup. (krb-00501)

12.012. View. (krb-00500)

12.013. View toward court.
(krb-00510)

12.014. Hallway. (krb-00512)

12.012

12.013

12.014

12.015. Courtyard. (krb-00499)
12.016. Courtyard. (krb-00506)
12.017. Interior. (krb-00514)

12.015

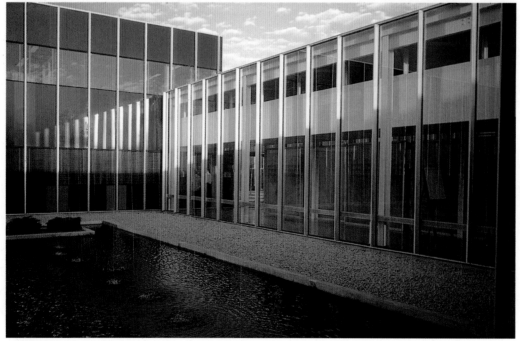

12.016

12.017

12.018. Office area. (krb-00518)
12.019. Office area. (krb-00517)
12.020. Offices. (krb-00519)

12.018

12.019

12.020

269

12.021. Mechanical detail.
(krb-00520)

12.022. Manufacturing area.
(krb-00521)

12.021

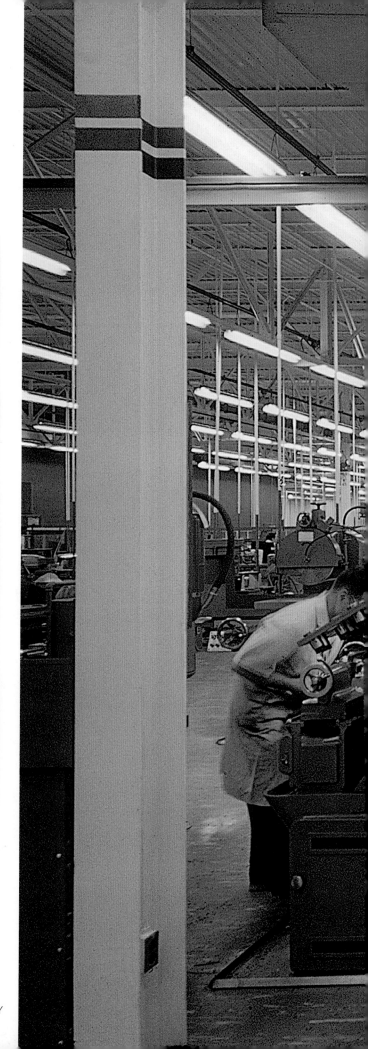

12.022

12.023. Cafeteria. (krb-00522)

12.023

12.024. Hallway. (krb-00527)

12.025. Hallway. (krb-00526)

12.026. Reception area. (krb-00525)

12.027. Hallway. (krb-00524)

12.028. View. (krb-00507) ➤➤

12.029. Entrance at dusk.
(krb-00496) ➤➤

12.024

12.025

12.026

12.027

13 IBM

THOMAS J. WATSON
RESEARCH CENTER

Yorktown, New York, 1956–61

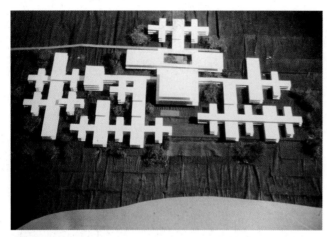

13.001

13.002

13.001. Study model. (krb-00530)

13.002. Model. (krb-00536)

13.003. Entrance. (krb-00529)

13.003

13.004

13.005

13.004. View. (krb-00539)

13.005. View. (krb-00540)

13.006. Entrance, detail. (krb-00538)

13.006

13.007. Office study model with photographer. (krb-00534)

13.008. Study model of hallway and offices. (krb-00537)

13.007

13.008

13.009. Hallway. (krb-00543)
13.010. Hallway. (krb-00541)

13.009

13.010

13.011. Cafeteria. (krb-00542)
13.012. Auditorium. (krb-00544)

13.011

13.012

14 YALE UNIVERSITY

DAVID S. INGALLS HOCKEY RINK

New Haven, Connecticut, 1956–58

14.001

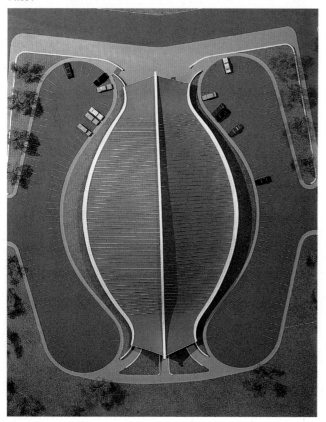

14.002

14.001. Model. (krb-00548)

14.002. Model. (krb-00549)

14.003. Entrance. (krb-00547)

14.004. View. (krb-00545) ➤➤

14.003

14.004

14.005

14.006

14.007

292 YALE UNIVERSITY: INGALLS HOCKEY RINK

15 TWA TERMINAL

JOHN F. KENNEDY
INTERNATIONAL AIRPORT

New York, New York, 1956–62

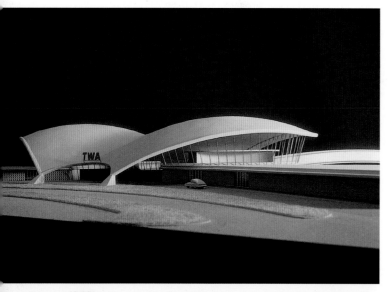

15.001

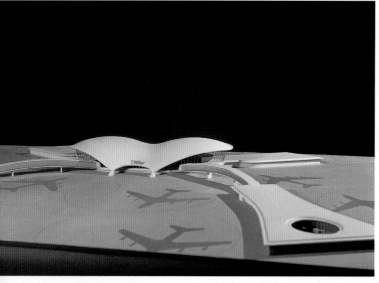

15.002

15.001. Model. (krb-00563)

15.002. Model. (krb-00562)

15.003. Entrance approach.
(krb-00558)

15.003

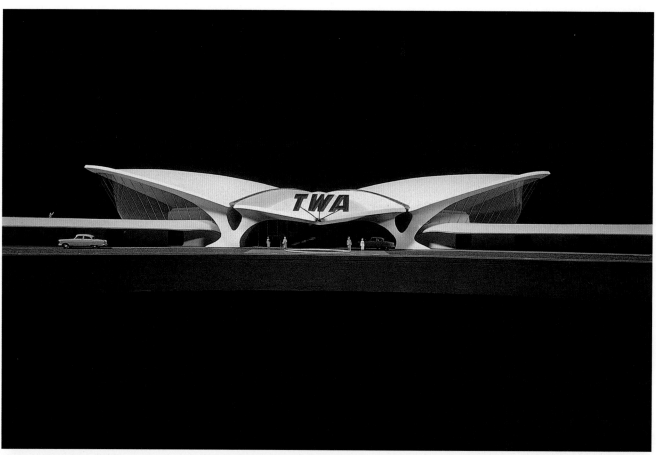

15.004

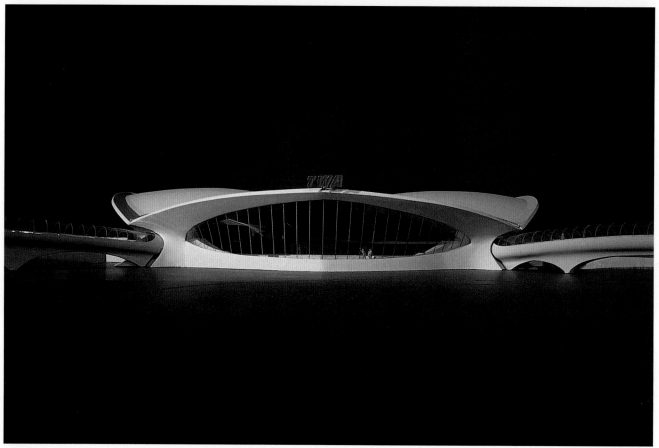

15.005

15.006

15.007

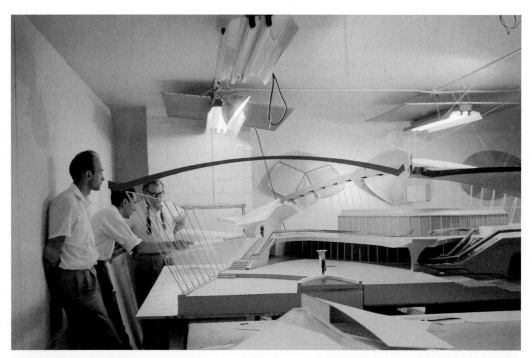

15.008

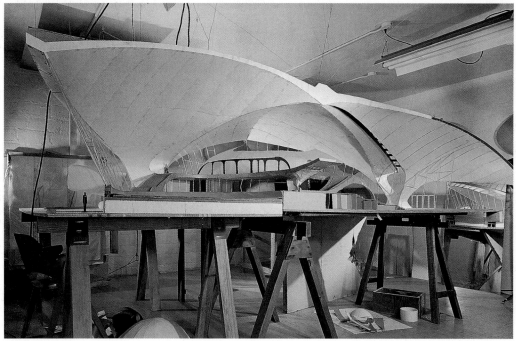

15.009

15.008. Model with office staff
and Eero Saarinen. (krb-00571)

15.009. Model. (krb-00575)

15.010. Model. (krb-00567)

15.010

15.011

15.012

15.013

15.014

15.015

15.011. Model. (krb-00587)

15.012. Model. (krb-00586)

15.013. Model. (krb-00583)

15.014. Model. (krb-00585)

15.015. Column studies.
(krb-00569)

15.016. Column studies.
(krb-00570)

15.017. Column studies.
(krb-00565)

15.018. Column studies.
(krb-00574)

15.019. Construction, detail.
(krb-00593) ➤➤

15.020. Construction, detail.
(krb-00591) ➤➤

15.021. Construction, detail.
(krb-00592) ➤➤

15.016

15.017

15.018

15.020

15.021

15.023

15.022. Construction. (krb-00604)

15.023. Construction. (krb-00598)

15.024. Interior. (krb-00622) ➤➤

15.025. Interior. (krb-00625) ➤➤

15.026. Interior. (krb-00624) ➤➤

15.026

15.028

15.027. Walkway. (krb-00616)

15.028. Information desk. (krb-00617)

15.029. Interior. (krb-00614) ➤➤

15.030. Interior. (krb-00606) ➤➤

15.031. Interior. (krb-00609) ➤➤

15.032. View at dusk. (krb-00600) ➤➤

15.029

15.030

15.031

15.032

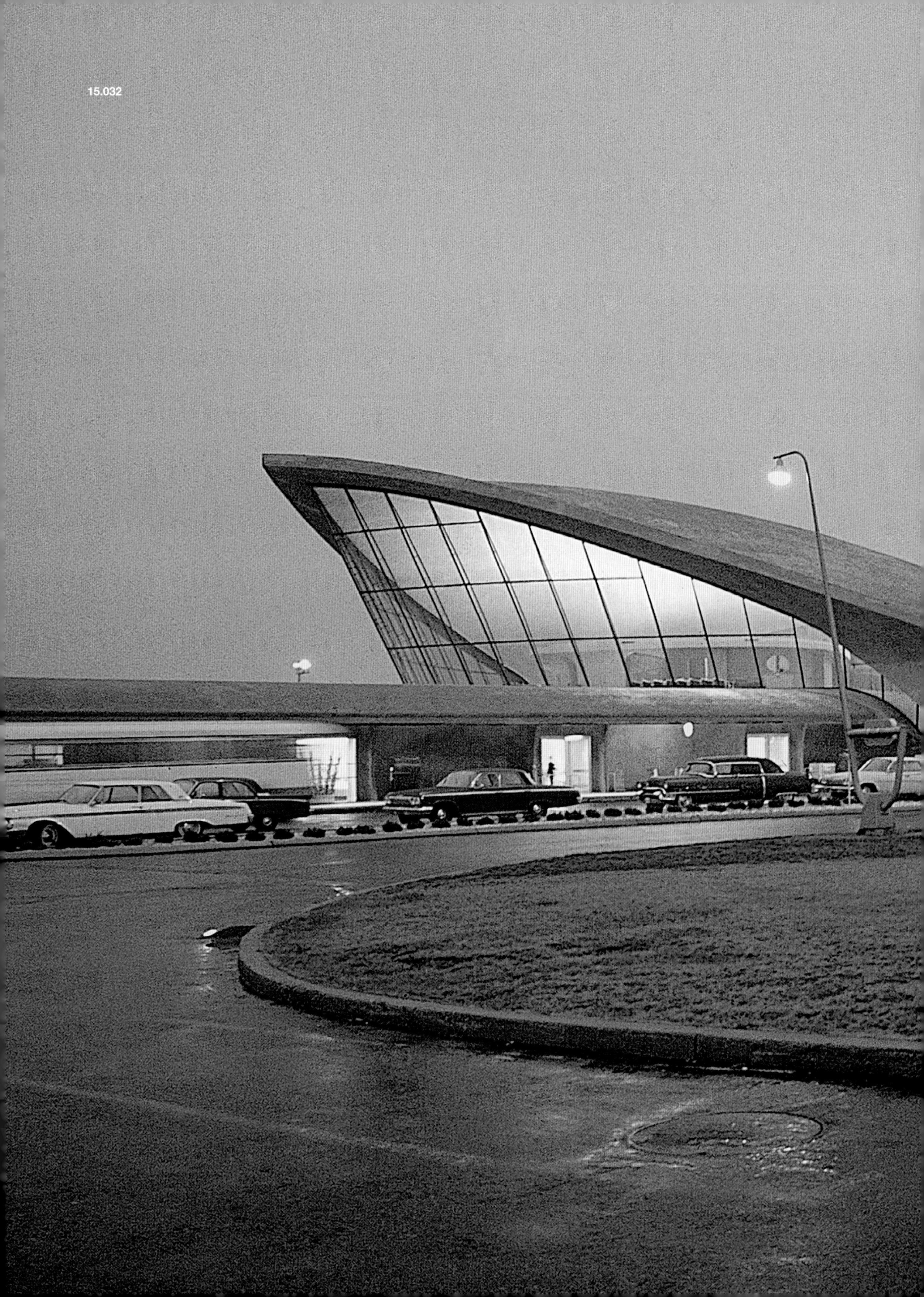

16 DEERE & COMPANY HEADQUARTERS

Moline, Illinois, 1956–64

16.001

16.002

16.001. View. (krb-00627)

16.002. View from lake. (krb-00628)

16.003. View from lake. (krb-00626)

16.003

16.004

16.005

16.004. Mockup. (krb-00631)
16.005. Mockup. (krb-00629)
16.006. View. (krb-00633)

16.006

16.007. Structural detail. (krb-00630)

16.008. Structural detail. (krb-00632)

16.010

16.009. View. (krb-00634)
16.010. View. (krb-00636)

16.011

16.012

16.013

16.013. View north toward auditorium. (krb-00648)

16.014. Wall detail. (krb-00658)

16.015. View east toward auditorium and exhibit pavilion. (krb-00639)

16.014

16.015

16.016

16.017

16.016. Exhibit pavilion. (krb-00640)

16.017. View east toward auditorium and exhibit pavilion. (krb-00638)

16.018. Administration building. (krb-00642)

16.018

16.019. Wall detail. (krb-00655)

16.020. Wall detail. (krb-00653)

16.021

16.021. Exhibit pavilion, detail. (krb-00652)

16.022. Administration, building detail. (krb-00651)

16.023. Administration, building detail. (krb-00649)

16.022

16.023

16.024

16.025

16.026

16.024. Administration building, detail. (krb-00645)

16.025. Administration building, detail with bridge. (krb-00646)

16.026. Administration building, detail with bridge. (krb-00643)

337

16.028

16.027. Offices. (krb-00663)

16.028. Office area. (krb-00664)

16.029. Entrance through exhibit
pavilion. (krb-00661) ➤➤

16.031

16.030. View from exhibit pavilion
toward administration building.
(krb-00666)

16.031. Exhibit pavilion, interior.
(krb-00665)

16.032. Executive reception area
at dusk. (krb-00667) ➤➤

17 YALE UNIVERSITY
MORSE AND STILES COLLEGES

New Haven, Connecticut, 1958–62

17.001

17.001. Aerial view. (krb-00699)

17.002. Courtyard view. (krb-00700)

17.002

17.003. View toward
dining hall. (krb-00690)

17.004. View toward
upper courtyard.
(krb-00691)

17.004

17.005

17.005. View toward Payne Whitney
Gymnasium. (krb-00703)

17.006. View. (krb-00707)

17.006

17.007

17.008

17.009

17.007. View. (krb-00702)

17.008. View. (krb-00704)

17.009. View. (krb-00705)

17.010. Sculptural detail. (krb-00706)

17.011. View. (krb-00708)

17.012. Wall detail. (krb-00709)

17.010

17.011

17.012

17.013

17.013. View. (krb-00712)

17.014. Construction with sculptor
Tino Nivola (left). (krb-00695)

17.015. Construction with sculptor
Tino Nivola (left). (krb-00692)

17.014

17.015

17.016

17.017

18 DULLES INTERNATIONAL AIRPORT

Chantilly, Virginia, 1958–63

18.001

18.001. Entrance approach. (krb-00714)

18.002. View. (krb-00713)

18.002

18.003

18.004

18.003. Model. (krb-00718)

18.004. Model. (krb-00724)

18.005. Model. (krb-00726)

18.006. Model with Balthazar Korab. (krb-00716)

18.007. Model. (krb-00717)

18.005

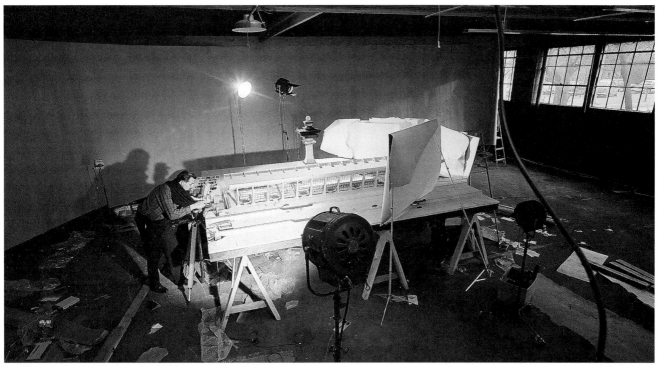

18.006

18.007

18.008

18.008. Model. (krb-00720)

18.009. Model. (krb-00719)

18.010. Model. (krb-00721)

18.009

18.011

18.012

18.013

367

18.014. Construction. (krb-00739)

18.015. Construction. (krb-00738)

18.016. Construction. (krb-00742)

18.014

18.015

18.017. Construction.
(krb-00736) ➤➤

18.018. View from runway.
(krb-00746) ➤➤

18.016

18.017

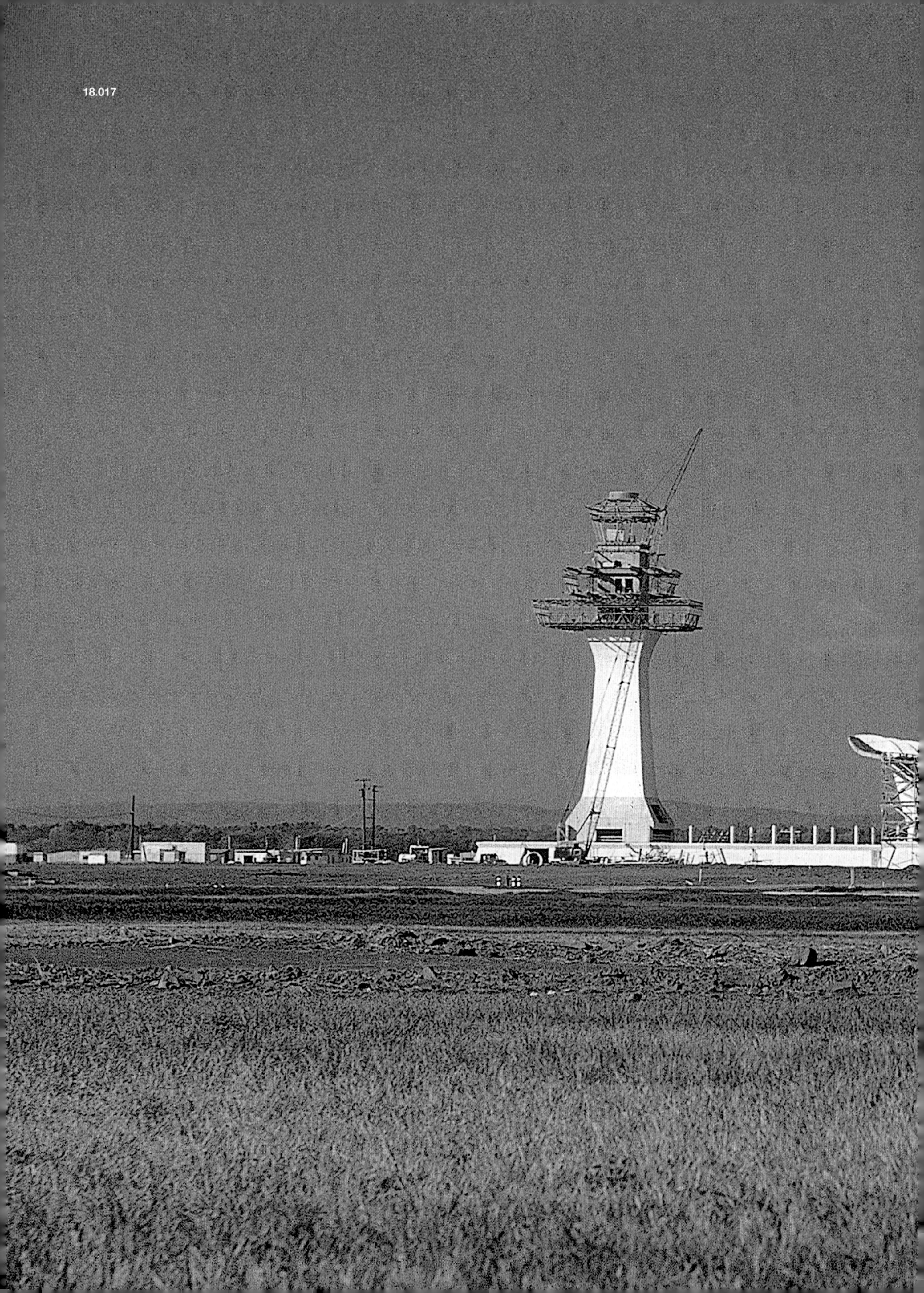

18.018

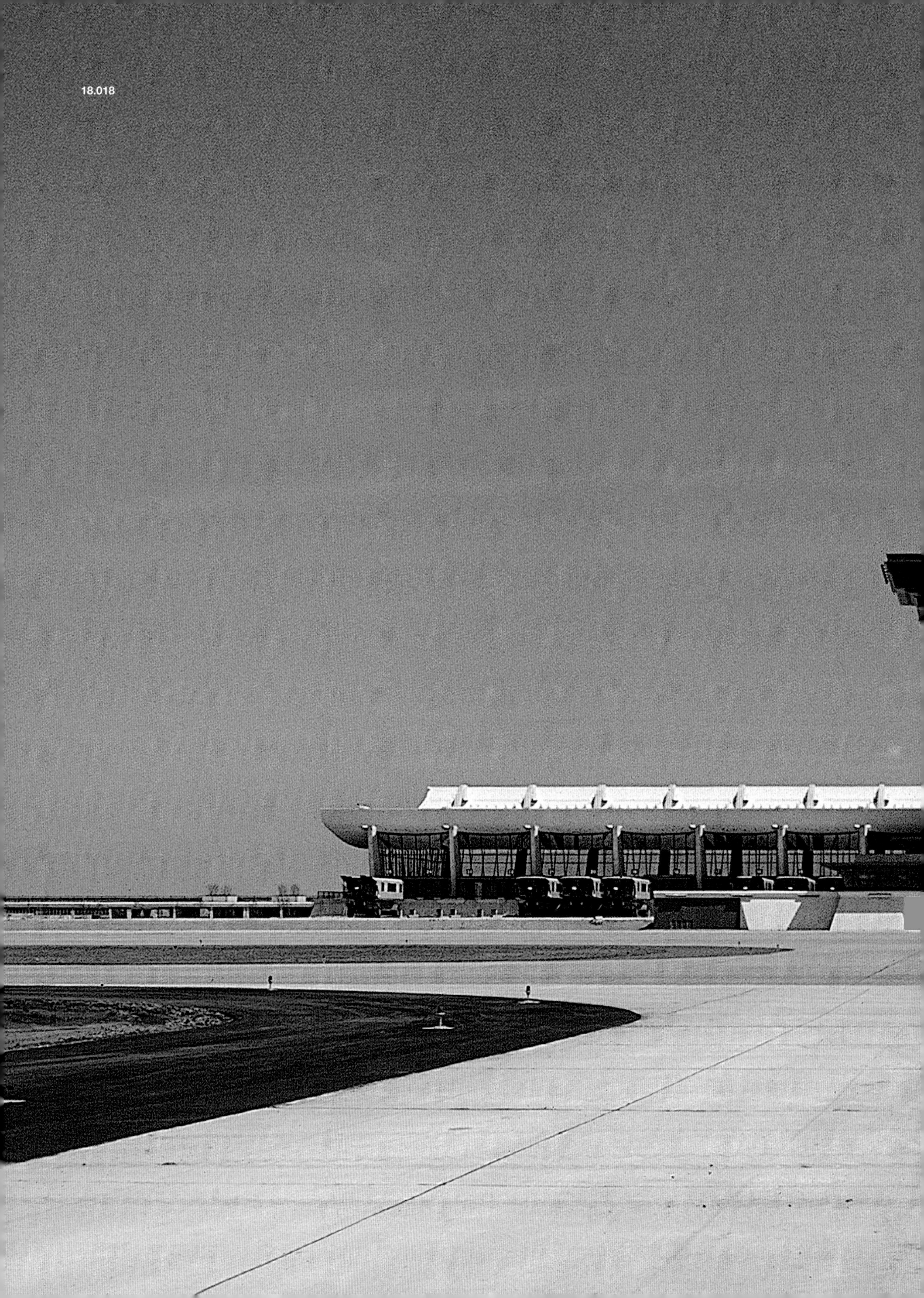

18.019

18.020

18.021

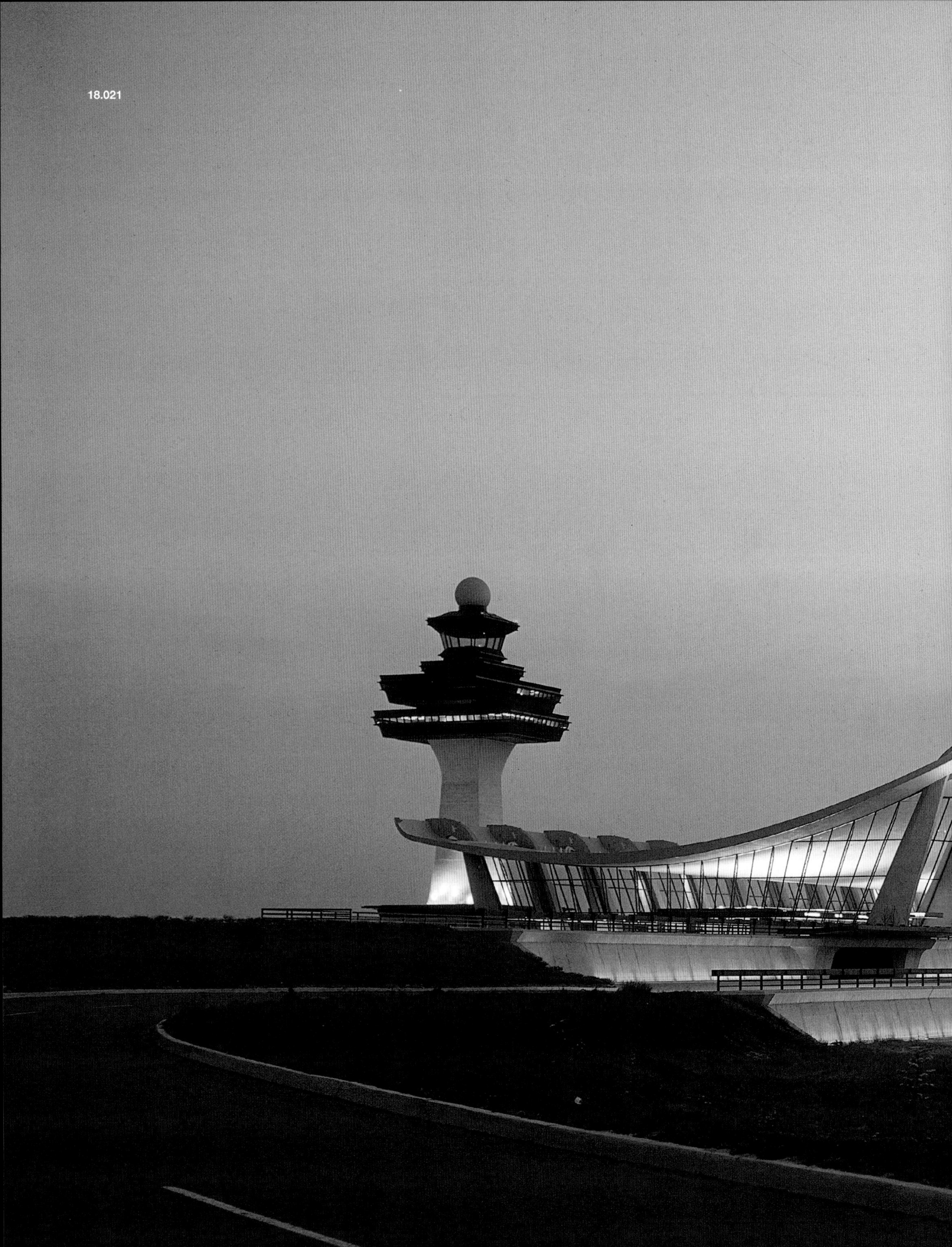

18.023. Column details. (krb-00762)

18.024. Column details. (krb-00766)

18.023

18.025

18.026

18.027

18.028

18.029

18.028. Interior with mural.
(krb-00795)

18.029. Interior with mural.
(krb-00794)

18.030. Extension construction.
(krb-00730)

18.031. Extension construction.
(krb-00734)

18.032. View with extension.
(krb-00797)

18.033. View with extension.
(krb-00800)

18.032

18.033

18.034. View with extension at dusk. (krb-00802)

18.035. View with extension at dusk. (krb-00798)

18.036. View with extension at dusk. (krb-00801) ➤➤

18.036

19 NORTH CHRISTIAN CHURCH

Columbus, Indiana, 1959–64

19.001

19.002

19.001. Aerial view. (krb-00803)

19.002. Aerial view. (krb-007804)

19.003. View. (krb-00810)

19.004

19.005

19.006

19.008

19.007. View. (krb-00808)
19.008. View at sunset. (krb-007813)

19.009. Interior. (krb-00816)

19.010. Interior. (krb-00815)

19.010

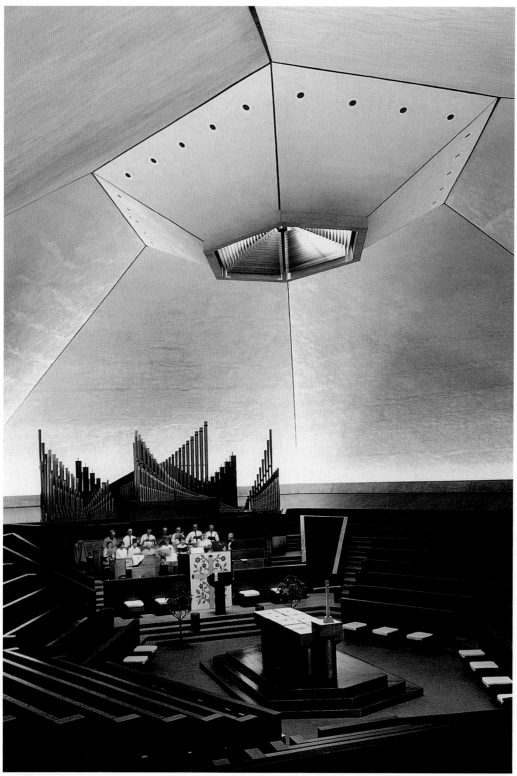

19.011. Interior. (krb-00814)

19.012. Skylight detail. (krb-00817)

19.013. Interior. (krb-00818) ➤➤

19.011

19.012

REMEMBERING EERO SAARINEN

THE BLOOMFIELD HILLS OFFICE, 1955–58

BALTHAZAR KORAB

On a December day of 1955, fresh over from Paris, I walked into the small Saarinen office in Bloomfield Hills with a beat-up box of 8x10s of my Beaux-Arts graduation work. "Can I see Mr. Saarinen? I'm looking for a job." He did see me, and having reviewed my prints, asked whether I could start that very afternoon—for $2.75 an hour pay. I did.

I remember every detail of that bizarre first American experience of mine and flash back to Taliesin, three years later, when the pay offered was one dollar a day. "The first time I've ever offered to pay anyone," insisted the old master. But that's another story.

Back to Saarinen's extraordinary workshop of some 20 people from all over the world. I myself experimented with a new instrument, the camera, often splitting my time, day and night, between my pencil and my Leica. My challenge was to protect a virtual reality from those random, designer-built studies or from the polished presentation models. The former task was the more exciting one. We developed a routine where the camera and the photographer became an integral part of the design process. The photograph became a visual test for the designer. We were intrigued by the extent to which Eero grew dependent on the images, particularly during the TWA studies.

Both form and space could be conveyed conveniently with my small Leica. Its size allowed access into the models where our view could not reach. Special theatrical effects such as images of real scenery projected for background and smoke and mirrors (literally) were used to enhance the impression of space. In presentations to clients, large-scale projection of slides conveyed the "being in it" experience. Slide shows eventually replaced the models themselves in our presentations. This was all before computer-generated imagery.

I wore two hats with some reservation. After all, I came to Saarinen to hone my Beaux-Arts training in Grand Design. A chance came with an invitation, from a dear Hungarian friend in Sydney, to jointly enter the Opera House competition. I accepted it, but since Saarinen was on the jury, I had to quit my job. While we worked on our design by correspondence (pre-e-mail), and an eventual flight to Australia to draw up the project, photography became my livelihood. As it turned out, I became an instant success in the field of architectural photography.

Our Sydney Opera design being a notable near miss, I rejoined Saarinen, earning a heightened appreciation and pay but still wearing two hats. Eventually, temptation from a series of major competitions including the Auschwitz Memorial and Toronto City Hall (with failure to win any) and my proven survival through my newly acquired craft, made me opt for a happily nomadic existence as a full-time photographer.

My newfound profession gave me a heady feeling of independence. An appreciation by the best and the brightest (such colleagues as Mies, I.M. Pei, Yamasaki, the TACs, the CRSs, the SOMs, the HOKs), my continued work with Eero for his sadly short remaining time, the Fraternity of the Saarinen connection (Rapson, Weese, Parker, Birkerts, Roche, Pelli, Kennon), new clients becoming old friends (William Kessler, Fay Jones, Edward Dart, John Macsai, Hugh Jacobsen, John Johansen, and many others), made it a rewarding involvement with cutting edge architecture.

It was the Saarinen role in the remarkable patronage of architecture in Columbus, Indiana, that made me part of the town history as their favored reporter.

The three magazines; *Architectural Forum*, *Record*, and *PA*, competed for my services. In one month in the early 60s I made the grand slam; cover stories in all three. Within five years in practice I scored the top award, the AIA medal for photography.

Forty years of worldwide adventure on the road, and in the process, launching new talents, including, proudly, my son Christian—all that made it well worthwhile for me.

Now at age 75, I stop for a moment to examine my body of work for quality and character. Will it leave a lasting value for the world on its own merits, beyond the honest service I was to offer to the cause of architecture?

I will let the world respond.

APPENDICES

ADDITIONAL PHOTOGRAPHS

01 GENERAL MOTORS TECHNICAL CENTER Warren, Michigan

01.069 (krb-00050)

01.070 (krb-00046)

01.071 (krb-00049)

01.072 (krb-00045)

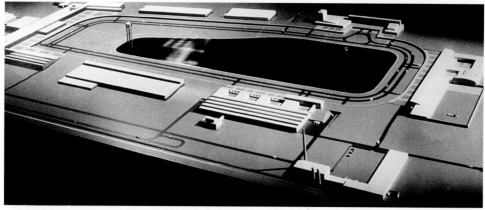

01.073 (krb-00043)

01.074 (krb-00058)

01.075 (krb-00055)

01.076 (krb-00062)

01.077 (krb-00065)

01.078 (krb-00068)

01.079 (krb-00070)

01.080 (krb-00071)

01.081 (krb-00085)

01.082 (krb-00084)

01.083 (krb-00082)

01.084 (krb-00075)

01.085 (krb-00078)

01.086 (krb-00087)

01.087 (krb-00061)

01.088 (krb-00056)

01.089 (krb-00063)

01.090 (krb-00091)

01.091 (krb-00118)

01.092 (krb-00108)

01.093 (krb-00106)

01.094 (krb-00107)

01.095 (krb-00100)

01.096 (krb-00116)

01.097 (krb-00104)

01.098 (krb-00136)

01.099 (krb-00140)

01.100 (krb-00144)

01.101 (krb-00152)

01.102 (krb-00151)

01.103 (krb-00150)

01.104 (krb-00132)

01.105 (krb-00133)

01.106 (krb-00129)

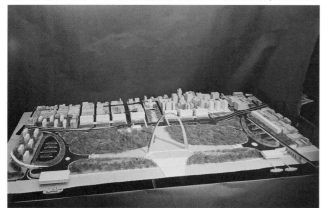

02.018 (krb-00156)

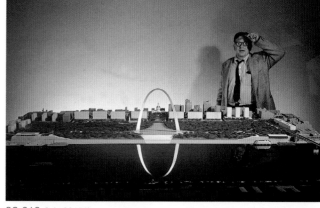

02.019 (krb-00159)

02.020 (krb-00172)

02.021 (krb-00182)

02.022 (krb-00180)

02.023 (krb-00166)

02.024 (krb-00170)

02.025 (krb-00175)

02.026 (krb-00171)

02.027 (krb-00176)

02.028 (krb-00154)

02.029 (krb-00169)

03 **MILLER HOUSE** Ontario, Canada

03.019 (krb-00189)

03.020 (krb-00187)

03.021 (krb-00185)

03.022 (krb-00192)

03.023 (krb-00188)

03.024 (krb-00195)

03.025 (krb-00193)

03.026 (krb-00206)

03.027 (krb-00205)

03.028 (krb-00212)

03 **MILLER HOUSE** continued

03.029 (krb-00213)

03.030 (krb-00210)

04 **IRWIN UNION BANK & TRUST CO.** Columbus, Indiana

04.015 (krb-00224)

04.016 (krb-00230)

05 **MIT: KRESGE AUDITORIUM** Cambridge, Massachusetts

05.022 (krb-00245)

05.021 (krb-00243)

05 **MIT: CHAPEL** Cambridge, Massachusetts

05.023 (krb-00251)

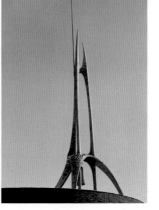

05.024 (krb-00253)

05.025 (krb-00260)

06 **MILWAUKEE ART MUSEUM** Milwaukee, Wisconsin

06.017 (krb-00275)

06.016 (krb-00266)

07 **UNIVERSITY OF MICHIGAN: SCHOOL OF MUSIC** Ann Arbor, Michigan

06.018 (krb-00268)

07.012 (krb-00291)

07.013 (krb-00300)

07.014 (krb-00299)

07.015 (krb-00281)

07.016 (krb-00301)

07.017 (krb-00297)

07.018 (krb-00298)

07.019 (krb-00296)

07.020 (krb-00295)

07.021 (krb-00308)

07.022 (krb-00305)

07 UNIVERSITY OF MICHIGAN: SCHOOL OF MUSIC continued

07.023 (krb-00309)

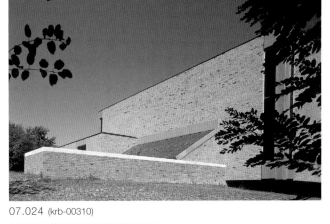

07.024 (krb-00310)

07.025 (krb-00303)

07.026 (krb-00304)

07.027 (krb-00311)

08 MILLER HOUSE Columbus, Indiana

08.041 (krb-00315)

08.043 (krb-00317)

08.044 (krb-00322)

08.045 (krb-00324)

08.046 (krb-00323)

08.047 (krb-00320)   08.048 (krb-00321)   08.049 (krb-00318)

08.050 (krb-00401)   08.051 (krb-00347)

08.052 (krb-00328)   08.053 (krb-00340)

08.054 (krb-00398)

08.056 (krb-00405)

08.057 (krb-00409)

08.058 (krb-00395)

08.059 (krb-00399)

08.060 (krb-00392)

08.061 (krb-00404)

08.062 (krb-00391)

08.063 (krb-00394)

08.064 (krb-00412)

08.065 (krb-00403)

08.066 (krb-00330)

08.067 (krb-00337)

08.068 (krb-00341)

08.069 (krb-00332)

08.070 (krb-00342)

08.071 (krb-00335)

08.072 (krb-00388)

08.073 (krb-00344)

08.074 (krb-00389)

08.075 (krb-00343)

08.076 (krb-00390)

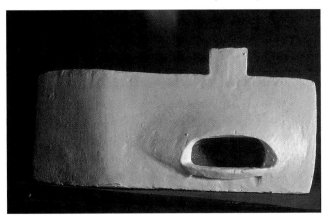

08.077 (krb-00369)

08.078 (krb-00362)

08.079 (krb-00364)

08.080 (krb-00368)

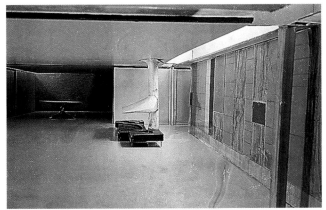

08.081 (krb-00363)

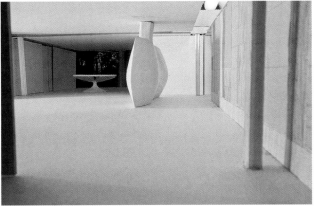

08.082 (krb-00365)

08.083 (krb-00360)

08.084 (krb-00357)

08.085 (krb-00356)

08.086 (krb-00358)

08.087 (krb-00361)

08.088 (krb-00353)

08.089 (krb-00376)

08.090 (krb-00354)

08.091 (krb-00385)

08.092 (krb-00380)

08.093 (krb-00371)

08.094 (krb-00349)

08 **MILLER HOUSE** continued

08.095 (krb-00386)

08.096 (krb-00383)

08.097 (krb-00375)

09 **CONCORDIA THEOLOGICAL SEMINARY** Fort Wayne, Indiana

09.015 (krb-00431)

09.016 (krb-00430)

09.017 (krb-00426)

09.018 (krb-00417)

10 **UNIVERSITY OF CHICAGO** Chicago, Illinois

10.007 (krb-00441)

11 **UNITED STATES CHANCELLERY** London

11.022 (krb-00455)

11.023 (krb-00449)

11.024 (krb-00451)

11.025 (krb-00456)

11.026 (krb-00467)

11.027 (krb-00454)

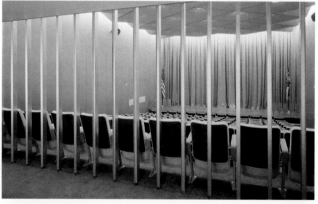

11.028 (krb-00478)

11.029 (krb-00463)

11.030 (krb-00461)

11.031 (krb-00452)

11.032 (krb-00462)

11.033 (krb-00468)

11.034 (krb-00445)

12 IBM: MANUFACTURING AND TRAINING FACILITY Rochester, Minnesota

12.030 (krb-00487)

12.031 (krb-00489)

12.032 (krb-00493)

12.033 (krb-00492)

12.034 (krb-00491)

12.035 (krb-00497)

12.036 (krb-00504)

12.037 (krb-00503)

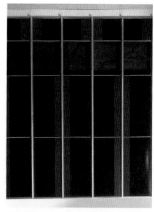

12.038 (krb-00485)

12.039 (krb-00498)

12.040 (krb-00495)

12.041 (krb-00494)

12.042 (krb-00508)

12.043 (krb-00523)

12.044 (krb-00516)

12.045 (krb-00515)

13 IBM: THOMAS J. WATSON RESEARCH CENTER Yorktown, New York

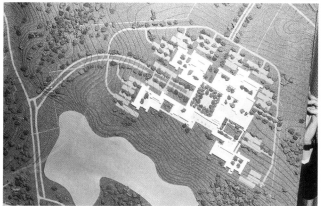

13.013 (krb-00531

13.014 (krb-00535)

13.015 (krb-00533)

13.016 (krb-00532)

13.017 (krb-00528)

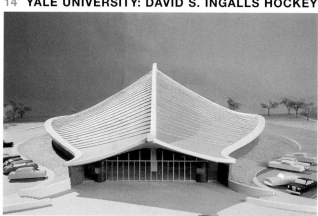

14.008 (krb-00550)

13.018 (krb-00513)

14 YALE UNIVERSITY: DAVID S. INGALLS HOCKEY RINK New Haven, Connecticut

14.009 (krb-00554)

433

14.010 (krb-00546)

14.011 (krb-00552)

15 TWA TERMINAL, JOHN F. KENNEDY INTERNATIONAL AIRPORT New York, New York

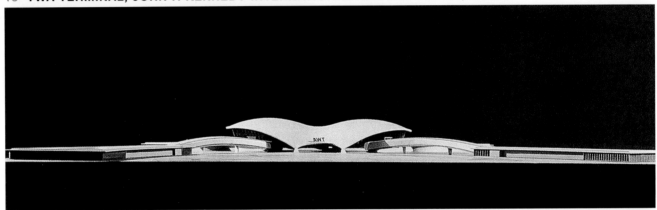

15.033 (krb-00564)

15.034 (krb-00579)

15.035 (krb-00566)

15.036 (krb-00568)

15.037 (krb-00557)

15.038 (krb-00572)

15.039 (krb-00576)

15.040 (krb-00573)

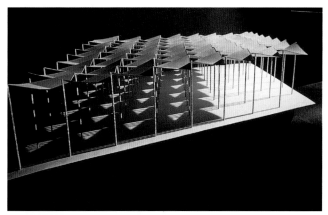

15.041 (krb-00559)

15.042 (krb-00560)

15.043 (krb-00596)

15.044 (krb-00590)

15.045 (krb-00603)

15.046 (krb-00595)

15.047 (krb-00594)

15.048 (krb-00589)

15.049 (krb-00597)

15.050 (krb-00588)

15.051 (krb-00599)

15.052 (krb-00601)

15.053 (krb-00584)

15.054 (krb-00821)

15.055 (krb-00623)

15.056 (krb-00620)

15.057 (krb-00602)

15.058 (krb-00613)

15.059 (krb-00615)

15.060 (krb-00607)

15.061 (krb-00608)

15.062 (krb-00610)

15.063 (krb-00611)

15.064 (krb-00577)

15.065 (krb-00578)

15.066 (krb-00618)

15.067 (krb-00619)

16 DEERE & COMPANY HEADQUARTERS Moline, Illinois

16.033 (Krb-00641)

16.034 (Krb-00659)

16.035 (Krb-00656)

16.036 (Krb-00657)

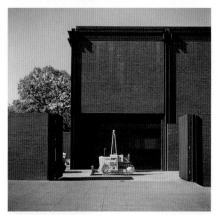

16.037 (Krb-00650)

16.038 (Krb-00654)

16.039 (Krb-00662)

16.040 (Krb-00660)

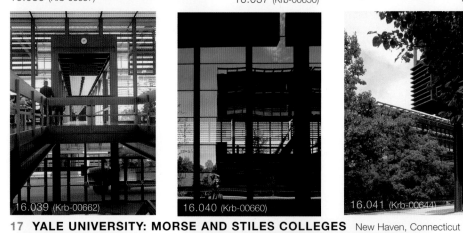

16.041 (Krb-00644)

16.042 (Krb-00647)

17 YALE UNIVERSITY: MORSE AND STILES COLLEGES New Haven, Connecticut

17.019 (Krb-00701)

17.020 (Krb-00698)

17.021 (Krb-00693)

18.037 (Krb-00722)

18.038 (Krb-00725)

18.039 (Krb-00723)

18.040 (Krb-00741)

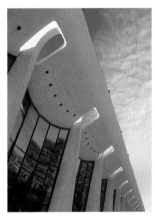

18.041 (Krb-00756)

18.042 (Krb-00735)

18.043 (Krb-00750)

18.044 (Krb-00754)

18.045 (Krb-00799)

18.046 (Krb-00737)

18.047 (Krb-00753)

18.048 (Krb-00751)

18.049 (Krb-00752)

18.050 (Krb-00759)

18.051 (Krb-00772)

18.052 (Krb-00745)

18.053 (Krb-00757)

18.054 (Krb-00781)

18.055 (Krb-00782)

18 DULLES INTERNATIONAL AIRPORT continued

18.056 (Krb-00779)

18.057 (Krb-00780)

18.058 (Krb-00792)

18.059 (Krb-00793)

18.060 (Krb-00791)

18.061 (Krb-00796)

18.062 (Krb-00747)

19 NORTH CHRISTIAN CHURCH Columbus, Indiana

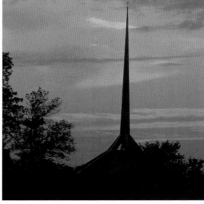

19.014 (Krb-00805)

19.015 (Krb-00811)

19.016 (Krb-00812)

BUILDING PLANS

01 GENERAL MOTORS TECHNICAL CENTER Warren, Michigan

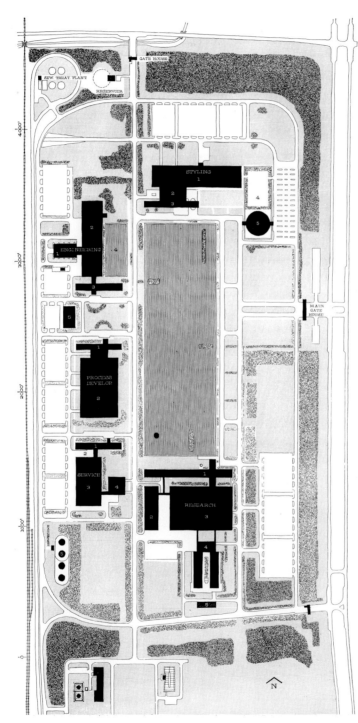

Site plan (ppmsca-15444)

STYLING
1. SHOPS AND STUDIOS
2. PENTHOUSE STUDIO
3. ADMINISTRATION
4. PAVED COURT
5. AUDITORIUM

ENGINEERING
1. DYNAMOMETER
2. SHOPS
3. ADMINISTRATION
4. REFLECTING POOL
5. RESTAURANT

PROCESS DEVELOPMENT
1. ADMINISTRATION
2. SHOPS AND FOUNDRY

SERVICE
1. ADMINISTRATION
2. DELIVERY COURT
3. SHOP
4. POWERHOUSE
5. FUEL STORAGE

RESEARCH
1. LABORATORY
2. METALLURGICAL
3. PROCESSING SHOP
4. MECHANICAL
5. FUEL BLENDING

Fountain is one of two in big rectangular lake around which the buildings are composed. This wall of water is 115′ wide, and shoots 50′ into the air, pumping 6,000 gal. per minute. Buildings beyond comprise the Styling Section. ⟫→

ARCHITECTS
Eero Saarinen & Associates
ARCHITECT-ENGINEERS
Smith, Hinchman & Grylls, Inc.
LANDSCAPE ARCHITECT
Thomas D. Church
GENERAL CONTRACTOR
Bryant & Detwiler Co.

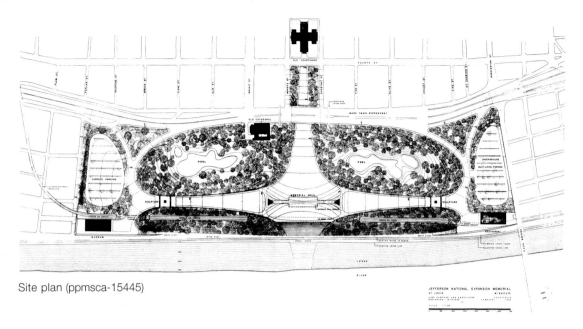

Site plan (ppmsca-15445)

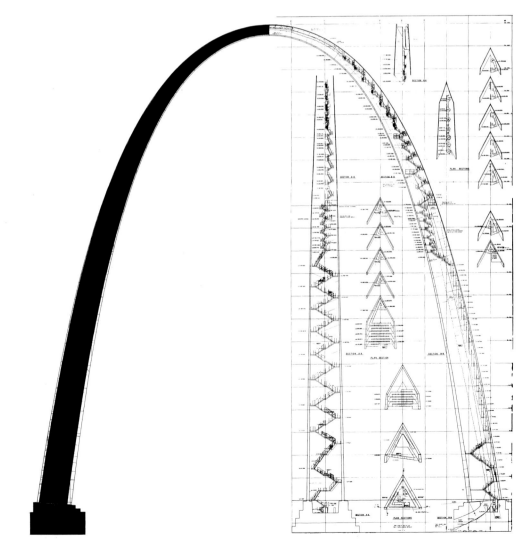

Section (ppmsca-15446)

03 **MILLER HOUSE** Ontario, Canada (ppbd-00352)

(Courtesy Will Miller)

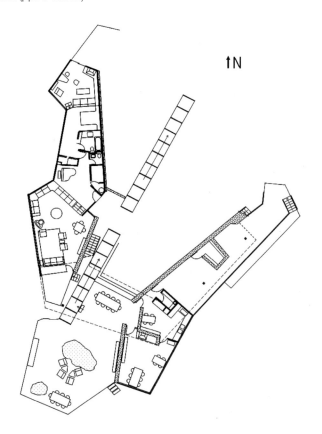

↑N

04 **IRWIN UNION BANK & TRUST CO.** Columbus, Indiana (ppmsca-15448)

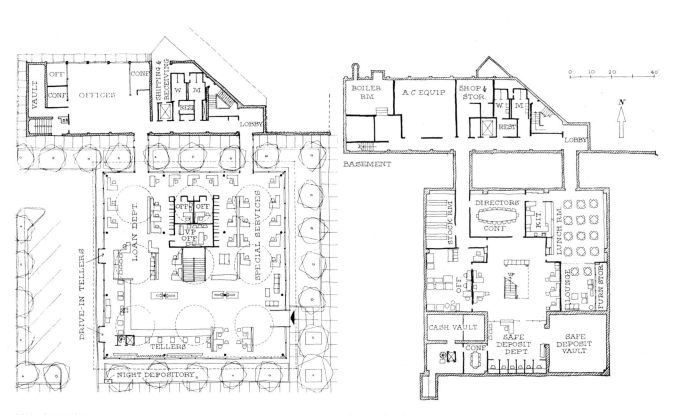

Main floor plan

Lower level plan

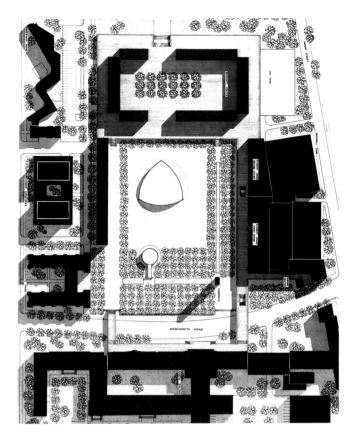

Site plan, Kresge auditorium and chapel (ppmsca-15449)

Section, Kresge Auditorium

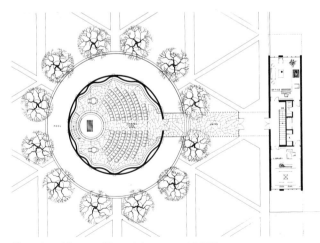

Site plan, Kresge Chapel (ppmsca-15450)

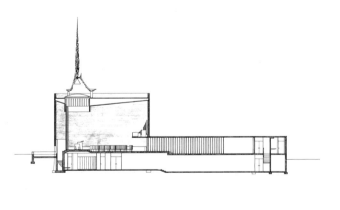

Section, Kresge Chapel (ppmsca-15451)

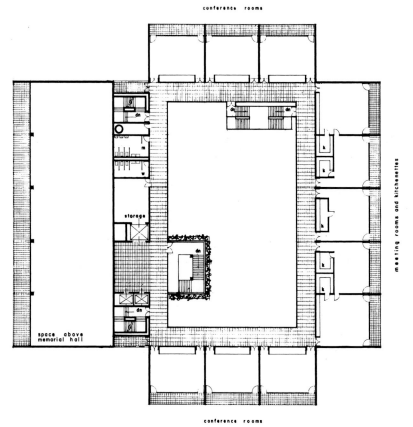

Second floor plan (ppmsca-15457)

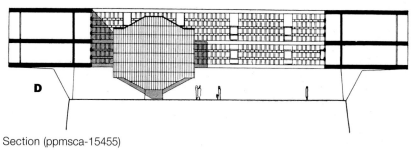

Section (ppmsca-15455)

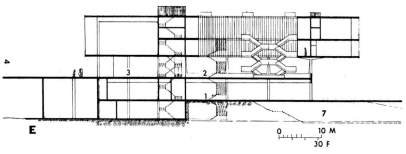

Section (ppmsca-15456)

Site plan (ppmsca-15453)

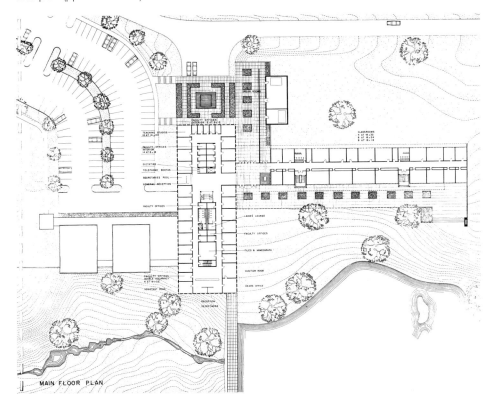

Main floor plan (ppmsca-15454)

08 **MILLER HOUSE** Columbus, Indiana *Architectural Forum* 109, no. 3 (September 1958): Floor plan, p. 129; Site plan, p. 31

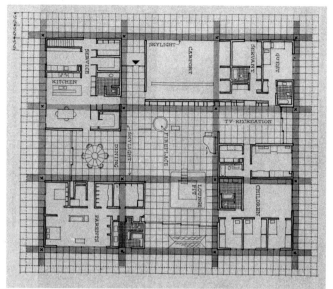

Floor plan (ppmsca-15493)

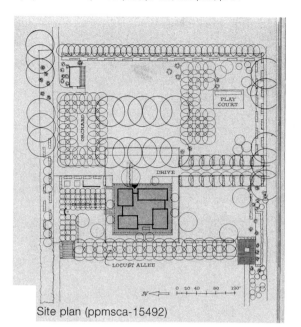

Site plan (ppmsca-15492)

09 **CONCORDIA THEOLOGICAL SEMINARY** Fort Wayne, Indiana

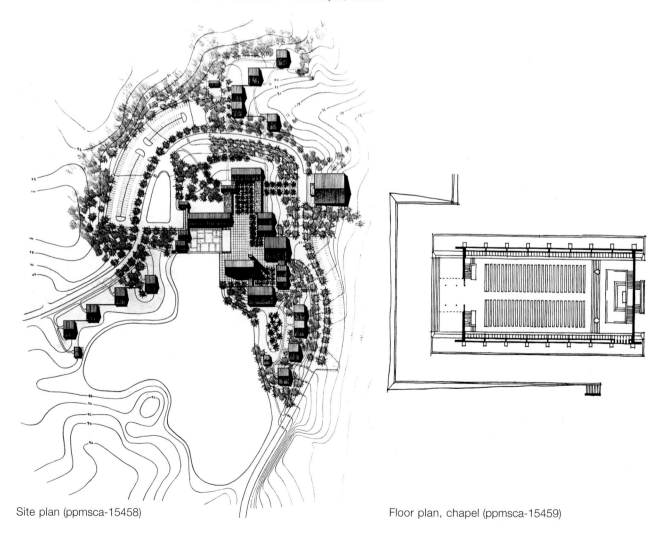

Site plan (ppmsca-15458)

Floor plan, chapel (ppmsca-15459)

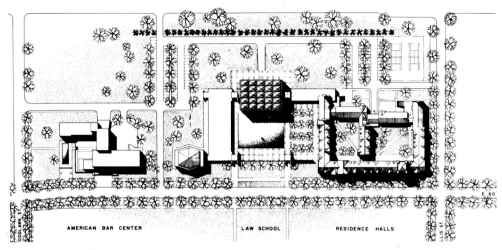

Site plan (ppmsca-15460)

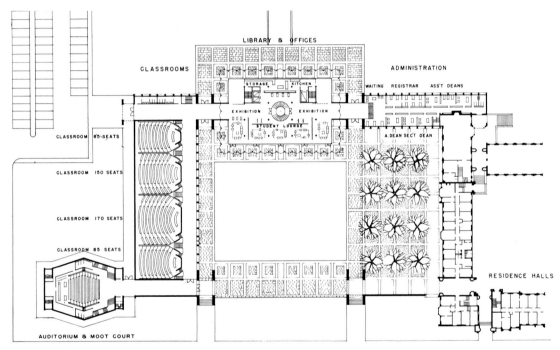

Main floor plan (ppmsca-15461)

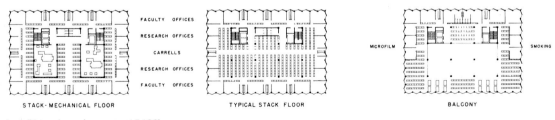

Typical floor plans (ppmsca-15463)

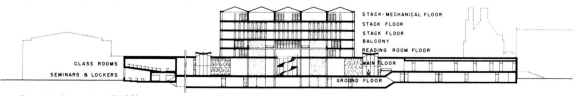

Section (ppmsca-15462)

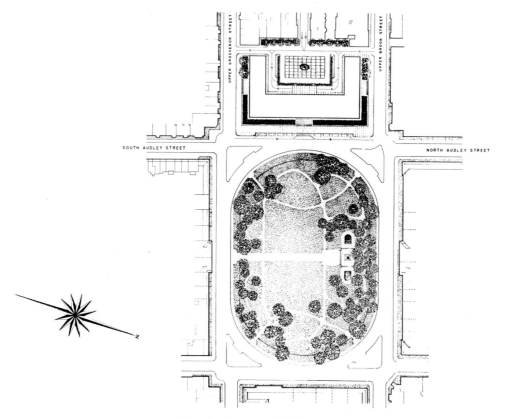

Site plan (ppmsca-15464)

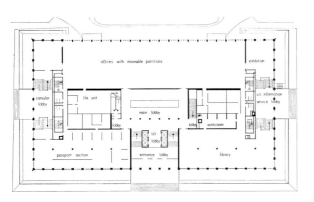

Ground floor plan

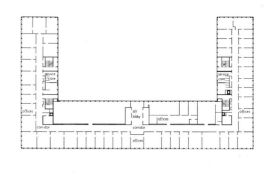

First floor plan (ppmsca-15466)

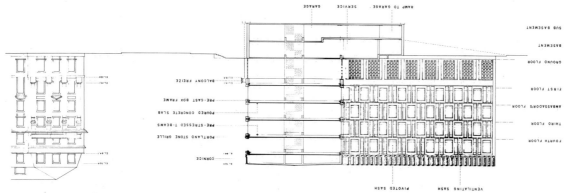

Section (ppmsca-15465)

12 IBM: MANUFACTURING AND TRAINING FACILITY Rochester, Minnesota

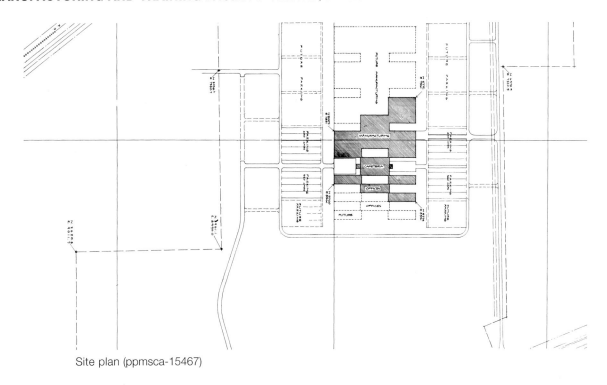

Site plan (ppmsca-15467)

13 IBM: THOMAS J. WATSON RESEARCH CENTER Yorktown, New York

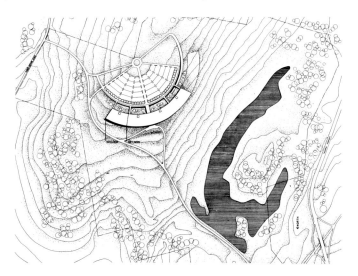

Site plan (ppmsca-15471)

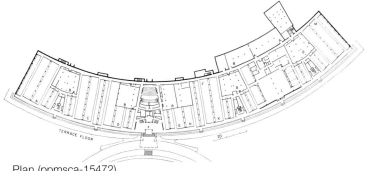

Plan (ppmsca-15472)

451

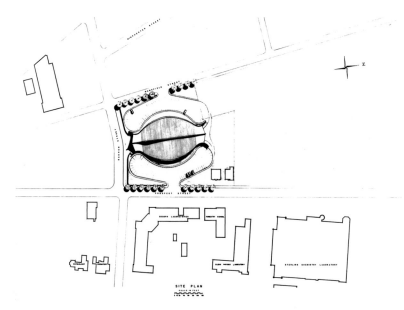

Site plan (ppmsca-15468)

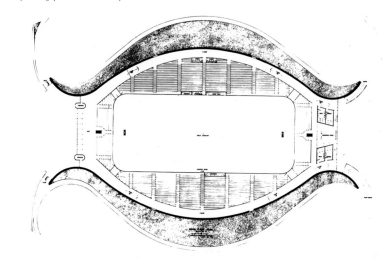

Plan (ppmsca-15469)

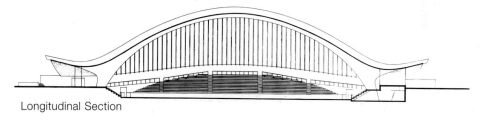

Longitudinal Section

Cross Section (ppmsca-15470)

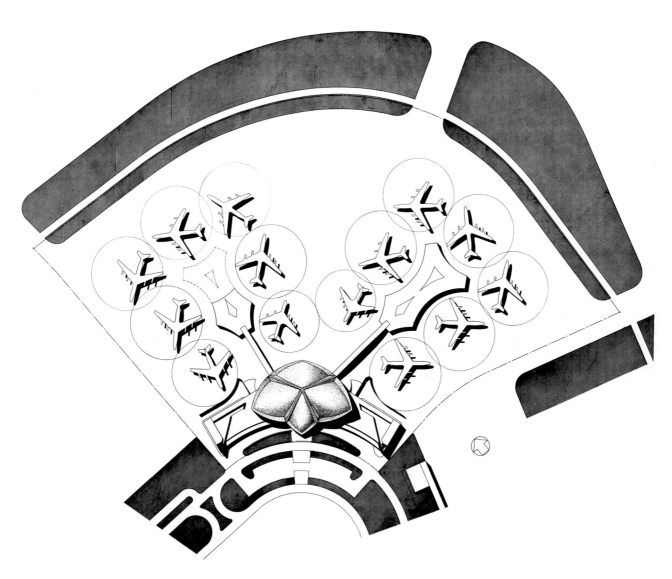

Site plan (ppmsca-15473)

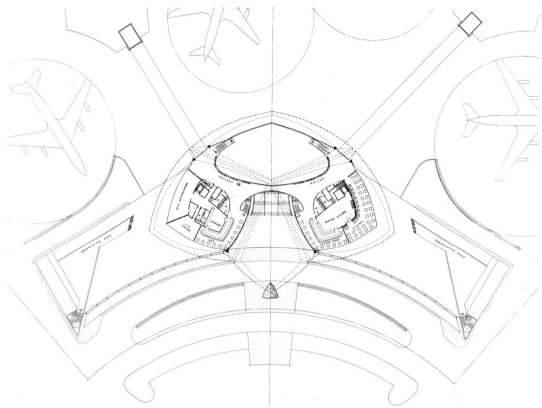

Upper floor plan (ppmsca-15475)

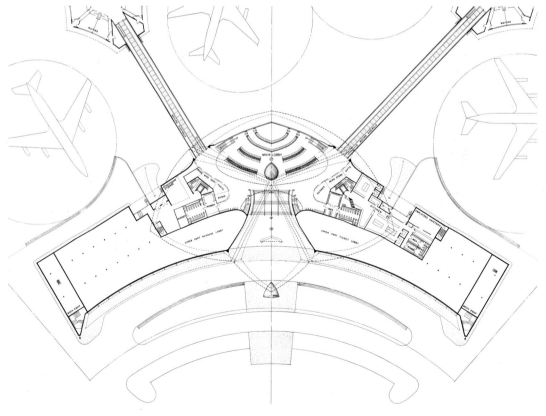

Main floor plan (ppmsca-15474)

Section through main lobby

Section through office wing (ppmsca-15476)

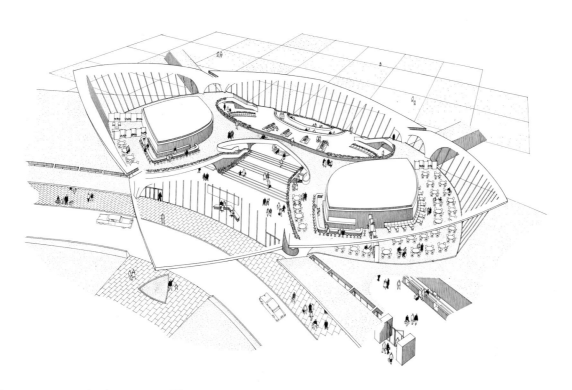

Cutaway perspective (ppmsca-15477)

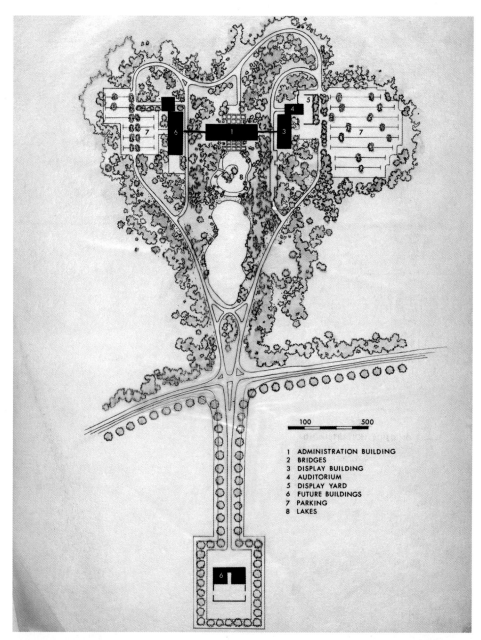

Site plan (ppmsca-15494)

1 ADMINISTRATION BUILDING
2 BRIDGES
3 DISPLAY BUILDING
4 AUDITORIUM
5 DISPLAY YARD
6 FUTURE BUILDINGS
7 PARKING
8 LAKES

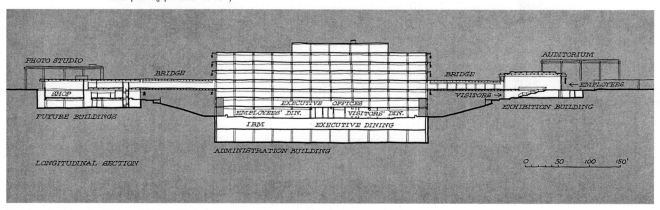

Section *Architectural Record* (July 1964): p.140, bottom (ppmsca-15480)

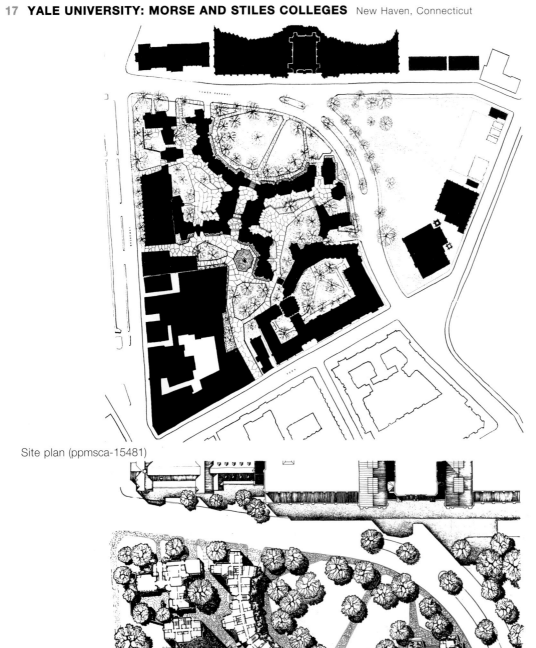

Site plan (ppmsca-15481)

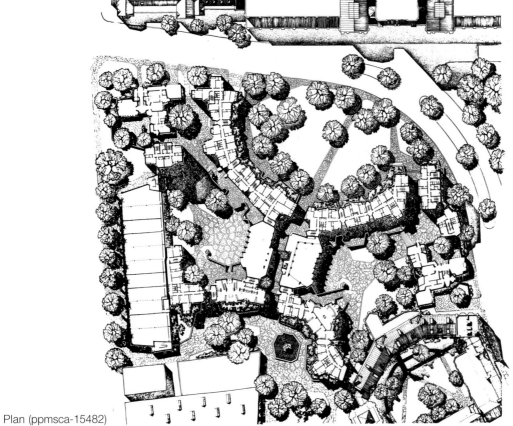

Plan (ppmsca-15482)

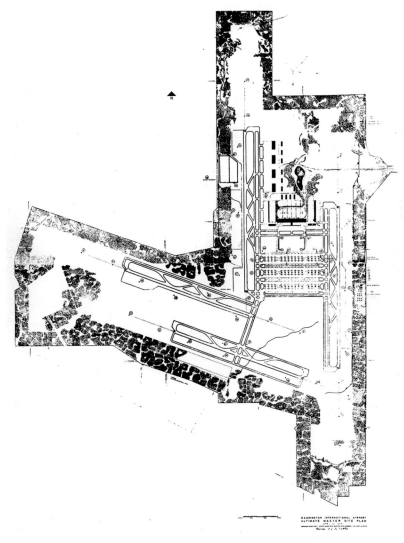

Site plan (ppmsca-15483)

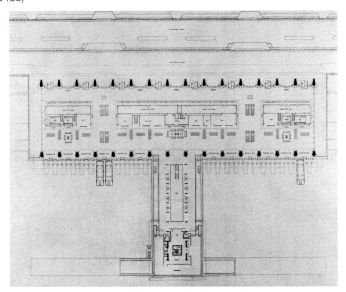

Plan (ppmsca-15484)

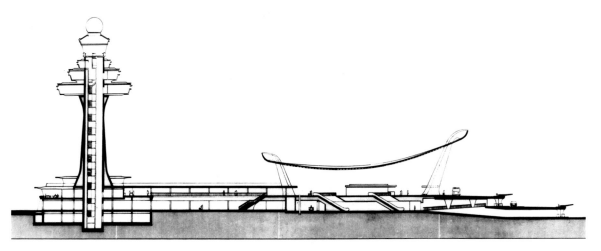

Section (ppmsca-15485)

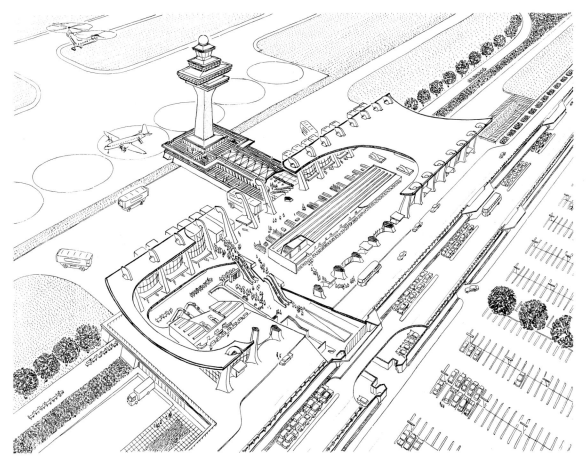

Cutaway perspective (ppmsca-15486)

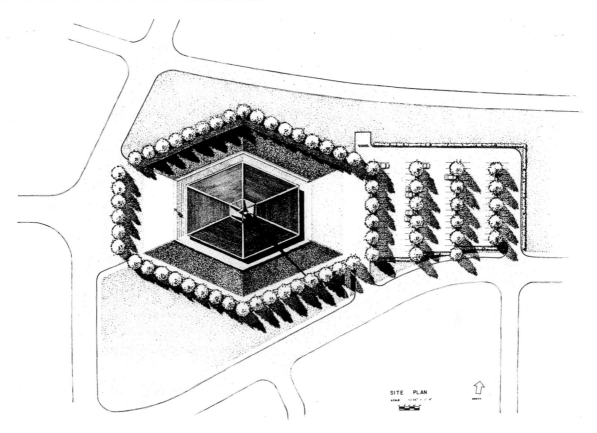

Site plan (ppmsca-15487)

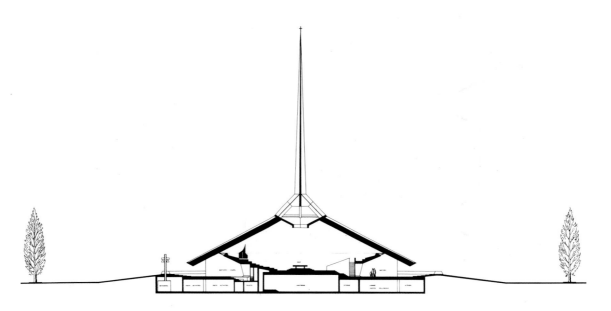

Section (ppmsca-15490)

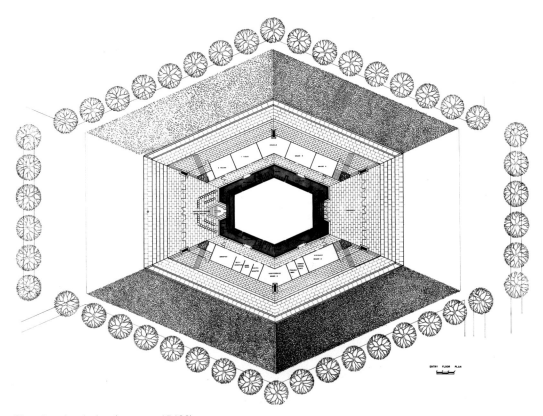

Church school plan (ppmsca-15489)

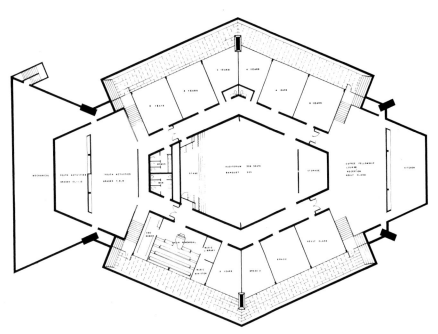

Main floor plan (ppmsca-15488)

BUILDINGS BY EERO SAARINEN AND HIS COLLABORATORS

This list is drawn primarily from research by Jayne Merkel (as published in "Buildings, Projects, and Furniture," *Eero Saarinen*; New York and London: Phaidon Press, 2005, 247-249); and from earlier, unpublished research compiled by R. Craig Miller (now Curator of Design Arts, Indianapolis Museum of Art). I am grateful to both for their kind permission to adapt their earlier compilations, and I take full responsibility for any errors or omissions my own list might contain.

As suggested by this list, and as advocated by his father, Eliel Saarinen, design for Eero Saarinen was very much a collaborative effort, and the degree of his contributions to individual designs cannot always be determined, as is true in many architectural practices today. Evidence for Eero Saarinen's involvement in each of the designs listed below—whatever that degree—is drawn from Merkel or Miller and, in some instances, supported by additional documentation in archives at the Finnish Museum of Architecture in Helsinki and the Cranbrook Museum Archives in Bloomfield Hills, Michigan. Reference should also be made to the recently published "Inventory of Buildings and Projects," edited by Donald Albrecht and Thomas Mellins, in *Eero Saarinen; Shaping the Future*, edited by Eeva-Liisa Pelkonen and Donald Albrecht (New Haven and London, Yale University Press in association with the Finnish Cultural Institute, the Museum of Finnish Architecture, and the National Building Museum, 2006, 120–221), . Designs for decorative arts, including furniture, are not included, nor are exhibition designs or student problems.

Interrelated commissions for single institutions, such as those for Drake University, are grouped together in a single listing; separate commissions for single institutions, such several for Yale University, are listed separately. – DDL

* An asterisk indicates a project featured in this book.

BEFORE 1937

Master bedroom, Saarinen House, Bloomfield Hills, Michigan (with Eliel, Loja, and Eva-Lisa—a.k.a. Pipsan—Saarinen), 1928–30.
Alterations to north wing, Hvitträsk, Kirkkonummi, Finland, 1928–33.
Helsinki Central Post Office and Telegraph building, Helsinki, Finland (competition entry; third place, unbuilt), 1934.
Swedish Theater addition, Helsinki, Finland (with Jarl Eklund and Eliel Saarinen; Saarinen design unbuilt), 1934–35.
The Forum (mixed-use commercial project), Helsinki, Finland (unbuilt), ca. 1935.
Finnish Pavilion for 1937 Paris Exposition (with Jarl Eklund and A.S. Sandelin; competition entry, unbuilt), 1936.
Cranbrook Institute of Science, Bloomfield Hills, Michigan, final design (with Eliel Saarinen, completing project initiated in 1931), 1936–37.

SAARINEN AND SAARINEN
1937–1939

"A Combined Living-Dining Room-Study designed for the Architectural Forum" (unbuilt), 1937.
Flint Cultural Center, Flint, Michigan (unbuilt), 1937.

Community House, Fenton, Michigan, 1937–38.
Koussevitsky Shed (originally Tanglewood music shed), Lenox, Massachusetts, 1937–38 (realized with modifications by Joseph Franz, 1939).
General Motors Futurama Building for the 1939 World's Fair, New York, New York (Norman Bel Geddes and Albert Kahn with Eero Saarinen, Caleb Hornbostel, Worthen Paxton, and others), 1938.
Goucher College, campus plan and library, Towson, Maryland (with Ralph Rapson and others; competition entry, second place, unbuilt), 1938.
Finlandia University, National Theater (formerly Suomi College), Lampeteer, Michigan, ca. 1938.
Wheaton College, Art Center, Norton, Massachusetts: (competition entry; fifth place, unbuilt), 1938.
College of William and Mary, National Theater, Williamsburg, Virginia: (with Ralph Rapson and Frederic James; competition entry, first place, unbuilt), 1938–39.
Crow Island School, Winnetka, Illinois (with Perkins, Wheeler & Will), 1938–40.
Kleinhans Music Hall, Buffalo, New York (with F.J. & W.A. Kidd), 1938–40.

SAARINEN, SWANSON AND SAARINEN
1939–1947

Smithsonian Art Gallery, Washington, D.C. (competition entry, first place; unbuilt), 1939.
First Christian Church (originally Tabernacle Church of Christ), Columbus, Indiana (with E.D. Pierre and George Wright Associate Architects), 1939–42.
"Demountable Space" Community House for U.S. Gypsum Company (with Ralph Rapson; unbuilt), 1940.
Cranbrook Academy of Art Museum and Library, Bloomfield Hills, Michigan, 1940–43.
Samuel Bell house, New Hope, Pennsylvania (unbuilt), ca. 1941.
Oberlin College, Hall Auditorium, Theater and Inn, Oberlin, Ohio (unbuilt), 1941.
Berkshire Music Center, Lenox, Massachusetts: Opera Shed (Theater–Concert Hall) and Chamber Music Shed, 1941.
Kramer Homes defense housing, Center Line, Michigan, 1941–42.
A.C. Wermuth house, Fort Wayne, Indiana, 1941–42.
"Unfolding House" project (unbuilt), 1942.
Willow Run war workers housing and town center plan, Ypsilanti, Michigan, 1942–43
PAC System for "Design for Postwar Living" housing (with Oliver Lundquist; competition sponsored by *Arts & Architecture*; first place; unbuilt), 1943.
Legislative Palace, Quito, Ecuador (competition entry, unbuilt), 1943–1944.
Lincoln Heights housing for National Capital Housing Authority, Washington, DC, ca. 1944.
Serving Suzy Restaurant and Gift Shop projects (unbuilt), 1944.
Gustav von Reiss house (unbuilt), 1944.
New Castle town center, New Castle, Indiana (unbuilt), 1944.
Antioch College, campus plan, Yellow Springs, Ohio, 1944–47 (with Max B. Mercer), 1944–45; Hugh Taylor Birch Hall dormitory, 1944–47.
Des Moines Art Center, Des Moines, Iowa, 1944–48 (from 1947, Saarinen, Saarinen and Associates).
Veterans' Memorial Building, Lapeer, Michigan (unbuilt), ca. 1945–46
Case Study House No. 8 (for Charles and Ray Eames), Pacific

462

Palisades, California (with Charles Eames), 1945–49; first proposal (unbuilt), 1945–48; redesigned and built by Charles and Ray Eames, 1949.

Case Study House No. 9 (for John Entenza), Pacific Palisades, California (with Charles Eames), 1945–49.

Drake University, Des Moines, Iowa, 1945–56: campus expansion plan, 1945–47; pharmacy building, 1945–50; dormitories and dining hall, 1945–55; theological school and chapel, 1952–56 (from 1947: Saarinen, Saarinen and Associates; from 1950, Eero Saarinen and Associates).

*General Motors Technical Center, Warren, Michigan, 1945–56; first proposal, 1945 (unbuilt); second proposal, 1946ff; final development, 1948–56 (from 1947, Saarinen, Saarinen and Associates; from 1950; Eero Saarinen and Associates with Smith, Hinchman & Gryllis, Architect-Engineers).

Birmingham High School, Birmingham, Michigan (unbuilt), ca. 1946.

Fort Wayne Art School and Museum, Fort Wayne, Indiana (unbuilt), ca. 1946.

Christ Church, Cincinnati, Ohio (unbuilt), 1946–48 (from 1947, Saarinen, Saarinen and Associates).

Detroit Civic Center (Riverfront Development plan), Detroit, Michigan (unbuilt), 1946–49 (from 1947, Saarinen, Saarinen and Associates).

Stevens College, campus plan, 1946–47; Chapel, first proposal, 1946–50 (unbuilt; from 1947: Saarinen, Saarinen and Associates); second proposal, 1953–56 (built), Columbia, Missouri (Eero Saarinen and Associates), 1946–56.

SAARINEN, SAARINEN AND ASSOCIATES
1947–1950

Christ Church Lutheran, Minneapolis, Minnesota, 1947–49 (alterations, 1956 and 1959, Eero Saarinen and Associates).

*Saint Louis Gateway Arch (originally Jefferson National Expansion Memorial), St. Louis, Missouri, 1947–65; competition entry (first place), Eero Saarinen with J. Henderson Barr, Alexander Girard, Dan Kiley, and Lily Swann Saarinen, 1947; completed with revisions, 1965; dedicated, 1968 (from 1950: Eero Saarinen and Associates with Dan Kiley).

Goethe Bicentennial Convocation and Music Festival, Music Tent (demolished), Aspen, Colorado, 1949.

Brandeis University, Waltham, Massachusetts, 1949–52: campus plan, 1949–52 (from 1950: Eero Saarinen and Associates with Matthew Nowicki); Ridgewood Quadrangle dormitories, 1949–50; Hamilton Quadrangle dormitories, dining, and social buildings, 1949–52 (from 1950: Eero Saarinen and Associates).

Yale University, Hillhouse plan and physics building (unbuilt), New Haven, Connecticut, 1949–53 (from 1950: Eero Saarinen with Douglas Orr).

EERO SAARINEN AND ASSOCIATES
1950–1961

Eero Saarinen house (alteration to 1860 dwelling), Bloomfield Hills, Michigan, ca. 1950.

Eero Saarinen guest house (originally Loja Saarinen house), Bloomfield Hills, Michigan, 1950–51.

*Miller house, Ontario, Canada, 1950–52.

Eero Saarinen and Associates office building, Bloomfield Hills, Michigan, ca. 1950–53.

*Irwin Union Bank & Trust Company, Columbus, Indiana, 1950–54.

*Massachusetts Institute of Technology, Kresge Auditorium and Chapel, Cambridge, Massachusetts, 1950–55.

*University of Michigan, North Campus plan, 1951–53 and School of Music, 1952–56, Ann Arbor, Michigan, 1951–56.

Time, Inc. Headquarters, various locations considered (unbuilt), 1952

United States Embassy addition, Helsinki, Finland (unbuilt), 1952.

*Milwaukee Art Museum (originally Milwaukee War Memorial), Milwaukee, Wisconsin, 1952–57 (completing project initiated in 1946).

Massachusetts Institute of Technology, Student Center, Cambridge, Massachusetts: (unbuilt), 1953.

*Miller house, Columbus, Indiana, 1953–57.

*Concordia Theological Seminary (originally Concordia Senior College), Fort Wayne, Indiana, 1953–58.

Vassar College, Emma Hartman Noyes House, Poughkeepsie, New York, 1954–58.

Greenwich Station, Greenwich, Connecticut (unbuilt), 1955.

United States Chancellery, Oslo, Norway, 1955–59 (with Engh, Quam & Kiaer).

*University of Chicago, development plan, Women's Dormitory and Dining Hall, 1955–58; Law School, 1955–60, Chicago, Illinois, 1955–60.

*United States Chancellery, London, England, 1955–60.

*IBM (International Business Machines) Manufacturing and Administrative Center, Rochester, Minnesota, 1956–58.

*IBM (International Business Machines) Thomas J. Watson Research Center, Yorktown, New York, 1956–61.

*Yale University, David S. Ingalls Hockey Rink, New Haven, Connecticut, 1956–58.

*TWA (Trans World Airlines) Terminal, John F. Kennedy Airport (originally Idlewild), New York, New York, 1956–62.

*Deere & Company Headquarters, Moline, Illinois, 1956–64.

University of Pennsylvania, Hill House College, Philadelphia, Pennsylvania, (originally Hill House Women's Dormitories), 1957–60.

Bell Telephone Corporation Laboratories, Holmdel, New Jersey, 1957–62.

*Yale University, Samuel F. B. Morse and Ezra Stiles Colleges, New Haven, Connecticut, 1956–58.

*Dulles International Airport, Chantilly, Virginia, 1958–63 (with Ammann & Whitney, Architect-Engineers, and Ellery Husted Associate Architect; expansion, 1998–2000, Skidmore, Owings, & Merrill).

Lincoln Center for the Performing Arts, Vivian Beaumont Repertory Theater, New York, New York, 1958–65 (with Jo Mielziner; Library-Museum of the Performing Arts above theater, Skidmore, Owings & Merrill).

*North Christian Church, Columbus, Indiana, 1959–64.

World Health Organization, Geneva, Switzerland (competition entry; second place, unbuilt), 1960.

CBS (Columbia Broadcasting System) Headquarters, New York, New York, 1960–65.

Athens International Airport, Athens, Greece, 1960–69 (with Ammann & Whitney, Architect-Engineers).

ABOUT THE DVD

The accompanying DVD contains printable, reference quality (low resolution) JPEG files of all the Balthazar Korab photographs in the book. With appropriate graphics software, the images can be used for study. Although the images are primarily intended for on-screen display, they also can be printed.

Further information about the image formats and rights pertaining to them can be found on the readme.txt file on the DVD and by going to the Rights and Restrictions Information page of the Prints & Photographs Division (http://www.loc.gov/rr/print/res/rights.html).

Almost all of the drawings by Eero Saarinen & Associates represented on the DVD were an unrestricted gift of Kevin Roche, and may be downloaded and used without permission. Higher resolution digital scans of these can be found through the Prints & Photographs Division Online Catalog (PPOC).

Exceptions include the drawings for the Miller Houses in Ontario, Canada (03), and Columbus, Indiana (08), which came from other sources.

The DVD includes a direct link to the Prints & Photographs Division Online Catalog (PPOC) (http://www.loc.gov/rr/print/catalog.html). The catalog contains over one million catalog records and digital images representing a rich cross-section of graphic documents held by the Prints & Photographs Division and other units of the Library of Congress. It includes most of the images on the DVD and many additional images, such as those in the HABS (Historic American Buildings Survey), HAER (Historic American Engineering Record), and HALS Historic American Landscape Survey collections. At this writing, the catalog provides access through group or item records to 7.75 million items, or about 56 percent of the Division's holdings.

SCOPE OF THE PRINTS & PHOTOGRAPHS DIVISION ONLINE CATALOG

Although the catalog is added to on a regular basis, it is not a complete listing of the holdings of the Prints & Photographs Division, and does not include all of the items on the DVD. It also overlaps with some other Library of Congress search systems. Some of the records in the PPOC are also found in the LC Online Catalog, mentioned below, but the P&P Online Catalog includes additional records, direct display of digital images, and links to rights, ordering, and background information about the collections represented in the catalog. In many cases, only "thumbnail" images (GIF images) will display to those searching outside the Library of Congress because of potential rights considerations, while onsite searchers have access to larger JPEG and TIFF images as well. There are no digital images from some collections. In some collections, only a portion of the images have been digitized so far. For further information about the scope of the Prints & Photographs online catalog and how to use it, consult the Prints & Photographs Online Catalog HELP document.

WHAT TO DO WHEN DESIRED IMAGES ARE NOT FOUND IN THE CATALOG

1. For further information about how to search for Prints & Photographs Division holdings not represented in the online catalog or in the lists of selected images, submit an e-mail using the "Ask a Librarian" link on the Prints & Photographs Reading Room home page or contact: Prints & Photographs Reading Room, Library of Congress, 101 Independence Ave., SE, Washington, D.C. 20540-4730 (telephone: 202-707-6394).

2. The American Memory site (http://memory.loc.gov), a gateway to rich primary source materials relating to the history and culture of the United States. The site offers more than seven million digital items from more than 100 historical collections.

3. The Library of Congress Online Catalog (http://catalog.loc.gov) contains approximately 13.6 million records representing books, serials, computer files, manuscripts, cartographic materials, music, sound recordings, and visual materials. It is especially useful for finding items identified as being from the Manuscript Division and the Geography and Map Division of the Library of Congress.

4. Built in America: Historic American Buildings Survey/Historic American Engineering Record, 1933–Present http://memory.loc.gov/ammem/collections/habs_haer) describes and links to the catalog of the Historic American Buildings Survey (HABS) and the Historic American Engineering Record (HAER), among the most heavily represented collections on the DVD.